Flashback

CRIME ETHNOGRAPHY SERIES

Series editors: Dick Hobbs and Geoffrey Pearson

Published Titles

Holding Your Square: Masculinities, streetlife and violence, by
  Christopher W. Mullins

*Narratives of Neglect: Community, regeneration and the governance of
  security*, by Jacqui Karn

*Families Shamed: The consequences of crime for relatives of serious
  offenders*, by Rachel Condry

Northern Soul: Music, drugs and subcultural identity, by Andrew
  Wilson

Flashback: Drugs and dealing in the Golden Age of the London rave scene,
  by Jennifer R. Ward

Dirty Dancing? An ethnography of lap dancing, by Rachela Colosi

Flashback
Drugs and dealing in the Golden Age of the London rave scene

Jennifer R. Ward

WILLAN
PUBLISHING

Published by

Willan Publishing
Culmcott House
Mill Street, Uffculme
Cullompton, Devon
EX15 3AT, UK
Tel: +44(0)1884 840337
Fax: +44(0)1884 840251
e-mail: info@willanpublishing.co.uk
Website: www.willanpublishing.co.uk

Published simultaneously in the USA and Canada by

Willan Publishing
c/o ISBS, 920 NE 58th Ave, Suite 300,
Portland, Oregon 97213-3786, USA
Tel: +001(0)503 287 3093
Fax: +001(0)503 280 8832
e-mail: info@isbs.com
Website: www.isbs.com

First published 2010

ISBN   978-1-84392-791-4 hardback

British Library Cataloguing-in-Publication Data

A catalogue record for this book is available from the British Library

FSC
Mixed Sources
Product group from well-managed
forests and other controlled sources

Cert no. SGS-COC-2482
www.fsc.org
© 1996 Forest Stewardship Council

Project managed by Deer Park Productions, Tavistock, Devon
Typeset by Kestrel Data, Exeter, Devon
Printed and bound by TJ International, Padstow, Cornwall

Contents

List of tables   *viii*

Acknowledgements   *ix*

1 Introduction: rave club culture   **1**
Ethnography   3
Theoretical foci   4
Introductory chapter and book content   6
Defining the terms   7
The UK rave club culture: an overview   9
Drug use among clubbing populations   11
Rave club drugs markets   14
Theorisations of rave club culture   16
My entry into studying the rave club culture   22
Key character introductions   25

2 Organisation of the London rave club scene   **31**
London rave club venues and events   33
Research sites and venues   37
Club London: a commercial rave dance nightclub   37
Lush: a small venue club night   39
Tylers: a small venue club night   42
Venus Group parties: a moving dance party organisation   44
The Pace Bar: a pre-club/DJ bar   47
Thrash parties: a free-party group   49
Summary   52

3   **Friendship network drug-use styles**   **54**
    Joe's free-party group and poly-drug use   55
    A group of young Australasians and heavy ecstasy use   56
    Andy: a sustained drug user   58
    Tom's group: an older group of clubber's drug use   59
    Extended clubbing sessions and drug taking   61
    Clubbing and increasing cocaine use   63
    Rave club lifestyles and health problems   67
    Mental ill-health and drug use   69
    Summary   70

4   **Drug selling in London rave clubs**   **72**
    Drug selling in nightclubs   73
    Andy and Joe as organisers of club selling   89
    Summary   90

5   **Social network drug selling**   **92**
    Robin as a social network dealer   93
    Joe as an example of a social network dealer   96
    Mick as a social network dealer   101
    Summary   106

6   **The role of women in drug selling**   **107**
    Women and front-line drug selling   109
    Women as assistants in nightclub drug selling   113
    Drug selling practicalities and assistance   115
    Women assisting in social network selling   117
    Women as free drug recipients   119
    Women as instrumental free-recipients   120
    Women rejecting drug selling partners   122
    Summary   124

7   **Scaling-up and moving out of drug selling**   **125**
    Drug purchasing on behalf of friends   126
    Convenience purchasing and subsidising recreational   129
       drug use
    Funding habitual drug use   132
    Naive recruitment   133
    Drug selling as a money-making enterprise   135

Looking after friends' drug selling businesses 136
Obstacles to moving out of drugs dealing 137
Summary 143

8 Later lives and conclusions **145**
Later lives 146
Recreational drug use and 'cultural normalisation' 149
Ecstasy and enterprise 150
Social network drugs markets and friendship 153
Rave drug market organisation 155
Drugs in clubs and security 156
Late-modern lifestyles and multiple identities 157
Where are we ten years on? 160

References 163
Index 176

List of tables

2.1	Club London: study period and main features	37
2.2	Lush study period and main features	39
2.3	Tylers parties study period and main features	42
2.4	Venus Group parties study period and main features	44
2.5	The Pace Bar study period and main features	47
2.6	Thrash parties study period and main features	49

Acknowledgements

Many people who in different ways assisted and supported me in producing this book require my thanks. First and foremost, these are friends I socialised alongside in the different friendship networks who enabled me to tell this story, and who made my years in this leisure culture the enormously fun ones they were. For reasons of confidentiality they will remain nameless. Special thanks go to Colin who introduced me to the rave club scene in the first place and who has continued to be a source of inspiration and encouragement of my academic study into it.

My PhD supervisor Professor Geoffrey Pearson requires special thanks for remaining keenly interested and helpful over the many years in which it took me to leave 'the field' and to get writing. Thanks are also extended to Professor Dick Hobbs and Professor Robert Power for their input into the book's content and especially to Dick for inviting me to publish with the Crime Ethnography Series.

A couple of people helped when my confidence was waning by reading and commenting on my manuscript which assisted me to keep going and reach completion. Dr Louise Ryan and Anthony Thickett require thanks here.

As well as thanks, some apologies are needed. These are to my friends and family who have experienced my absence in different ways, and maybe when it was needed, while I prioritised my ambition of completing a book. Special thanks go to Nick Kemp whose patience and support throughout the years of my completing the PhD, and again in turning the document into a manuscript have been tireless. Thank you.

Chapter 1

Introduction: rave club culture

For British youth ecstasy has become a milestone on the road
to adulthood like cutting your teeth, riding a bike and losing
your virginity. (Wright 1998: 231)

An exaggeration? Maybe, but it was without doubt that the
emergence of the rave club culture in the UK in the late 1980s,
and its ongoing transformations throughout the 1990s had a major
impact on the drug taking behaviour of British youth (Gilman
1991, 1994; Newcombe 1991; McDermott 1993; Collin 1997). Going
out 'clubbing' and taking drugs became a regular feature of many
young peoples' lives. It could safely be stated that by the mid 1990s
drug use in the UK was widespread (Collin 1997). An array of drugs
made up people's drug using repertoires, though 'ecstasy' and later
cocaine were by far the most popular (Riley and Hayward 2004). A
knock-on effect of this widespread drugs consumption was the large
numbers of people who became involved in selling them. Whether
they perceived themselves to be drug dealing or not, many people's
selling activities were at a frequency and level which constituted
'dealing'.

This book is informed by an ethnographic study of drugs use and
drugs dealing as it occurred within different leisure venues and
among different friendship networks participating in the London
rave club culture. The research was carried out over a five-year
period from the mid to late 1990s (1993–1998). Participant observation

techniques were employed to conduct the study; a style that took the author out socialising in numerous London nightclubs, dance parties, house parties, 'chill-out' sessions, 'after-club' parties, bars and pubs, people's houses, and among interconnected friendship networks where drugs were being bought and sold, consumed and discussed. From this lengthy and detailed investigation, unique insights were gained into drug selling in London's clubland and the careful organisation and interactions that surrounded the supply and trade in ecstasy and other dance drugs.

Various studies have examined aspects of this leisure culture, such as the significance and meaning it played in the lives of those involved, yet little work has paid attention to the income generation and economic activity connected to it. This book fills this gap. It focuses on the organisational features of drug selling and purchasing in different settings and social arenas and emphasises the enterprise and entrepreneurship that underpinned this activity. Rave club participants are illustrated as capitalising on the money-making opportunities generated through the widespread demand for drugs from within this leisure culture.

Drug selling is differentiated by trade in the more risky public domain such as in nightclubs and dance parties, and in the safer confines of the private domain, among extended networks of social and friendship group contacts. Different people are focused upon to highlight the various positions and roles they occupied in the drug selling and distribution process.

The camaraderie that supported rave club participation greatly assisted drug selling activities to expand; sometimes into thriving commercial operations. Friends put friends in touch with people they knew who were dealers, and people nurtured useful social contacts that aligned them to a drug supply. This was added to by the busy nature of the London urban setting which provided multiple contacts and assisted drugs trading activity to be disguised within its general lively milieu and vibrant form.

The book concludes with the argument that the construct of 'friends' was a useful one to adopt, in that it neutralised drug selling operations so they could be conceived of instead as set-ups that provided for friends' drugs needs. When scrutinised more closely, friends were often great in number and were sometimes people met in a club the night before, and whom the seller barely knew.

This ethnographic study makes an important contribution to the existing body of information on drugs market organisation, and makes a significant addition to the so far limited evidence base of recreational drugs markets.

Ethnography

The term ethnography is assigned to many types of qualitative research, and ethnographic studies exist in numerous forms (Pearson 1992; Armstrong 1993; Hobbs 2001). My style follows in the tradition of ethnographies emanating from the 'Chicago School' of the 1930s and 1940s. This approach has its roots in anthropology and applies the technique of participant observation to better understand the social and cultural milieu that people's lives are lived out within. The method elicits detailed information by being immersed in a social setting for an extended time period, locating oneself as close to the activity as possible in order to develop a deep understanding of the culture, the group, or the community under study (Hobbs and May 1993; Hammersley and Atkinson 1995; Bryman 2001).

Ethnographic participant observation is a highly relevant method in the study of illicit drug use and drugs dealing populations (Power 1989). Due to their illegal nature these are commonly concealed activities and detail surrounding their occurrence can be difficult to obtain. An effective way of attaining information is to become immersed in the drug user's social world where the actions of users and sellers can be observed at close hand. There are some well-known drugs ethnographies which have employed the Chicago School style of research and which provide rich insights into the workings of illicit drug markets and scenes. Some of the earlier classics include Becker's famous study of marijuana users (1953), and Polsky's study of the Greenwich Village 'beat scene' (1967 [1998]).[1] These classic studies have been the influence behind a number of other insightful ethnographies of drug selling set-ups in the latter part of the twentieth century.[2] (Rosenbaum 1981; Adler 1985; Williams 1989; Waldorf et al. 1991; Taylor 1993; Bourgois 1995; Maher 1997; Jacobs 1999; Pearson 2001, among others).

My research follows in the ethnographic tradition of the Chicago School. It involved immersing myself within the London rave club culture, over an extended time period, from where the social interactions and processes at the heart of club floor and social network drug selling operations were observed.

The study is distinct in that there has not been an ethnographic account of the ecstasy drug-using culture and economy. There

3

are ethnographies of street-level heroin and crack cocaine using and selling scenes, and social network observations of cocaine-using groups, which provide valuable insights into drugs market organisation. Yet to date there is not an ethnography of the ecstasy drug culture and the drug distribution systems that accompany it. There are Silverstone's (2003) and Sanders' (2005, 2006) ethnographies undertaken as members of staff within the walls of the London nightclubs they worked. From this they provide vivid detail of the interplay between nightclub security staff and ecstasy and cocaine selling operations. My work is an ethnographic account set in different rave club venues, among overlapping friendship networks, and was carried out over an extended time period. From this a rare view is offered into the processes and interactions that underpinned nightclub drug selling and social network dealing arrangements, and in this way it fills a vital gap in knowledge of rave club and recreational drugs markets.

Theoretical foci

The field observations of rave club drugs trading are analysed within a drugs market framework. This enables links to previous research, such as the way drug distribution systems have been conceived of as 'open' and 'closed' systems of operation, typically connected to ease of access to the individual (Edmunds *et al.* 1996; May *et al.* 2000; May and Hough 2004). These conceptions have mostly been applied to street-level heroin and crack cocaine scenes. Nonetheless they have applicability to this recreational drugs market.

'Open' drugs markets are defined as fixed-site geographical locations open to any buyer, with no need for prior introduction to the seller, and carrying few other barriers to access. Closed markets are ones in which access is limited to known and trusted participants (Edmunds *et al.* 1996). In recognition at the growth in nightclub and pub-based drug selling alongside the rave club culture, May *et al.* (2000) defined a third system sitting astride open and closed systems. These were referred to as 'semi-open' systems of operation where sellers would generally do business in the absence of a prior introduction, provided the 'buyer looks the part' (May *et al.* 2000: 6).

A similar differentiation to the open and closed conceptualisation can be drawn in relation to the rave club drugs market I studied. There was not an open street-level market where dance drugs could be bought. Instead, nightclubs provided this 'open' marketplace. Within nightclubs ecstasy tablets and other dance drugs could be purchased without restraint by the general drug taking population. At the time of my research it was possible to turn up at any rave club in the capital and be guaranteed a supply of ecstasy tablets. Anyone, providing they didn't look like an undercover police officer could purchase.

Drug selling within social and friendship networks could be conceived of as 'closed' systems where sales were restricted to familiar and trusted individuals, though as I will go on to point out, social network drug selling was in fact a relatively open system of distribution. These two definitions frame the drugs dealing set-ups observed in my study.

In addition to this broad drugs market framework the central themes of enterprise and entrepreneurship, friendship and functionality and the London urban setting, underline the analysis. A key theme running through this book is the enterprising nature of rave club participants. It is argued they were economic actors who seized both the legal and illegal money-making opportunities generated through this leisure culture. Rave club participants capitalised on the widespread demand for drugs by becoming involved in the sale and purchase of them. Moreover, they tapped into the legal economic opportunities being generated through this expanding night-time culture, by becoming leisure entrepreneurs running nightclubs and working as DJs. In this way they could be viewed as active economic agents involved in the production of the culture and economy of which they were a part.

A related concept is the way drug selling set-ups functioned as 'alternate work' and meaningful activity, and these themes have been applied in other studies of drug selling (Preble and Casey 1969; Adler 1985; Johnson *et al.* 1985, 2000; Williams 1989; Waldorf *et al.* 1991; Bourgois 1995; Ruggiero and South 1995, 1997, among others). Some of the characters I write about had left school with few qualifications and lacked skills to enter the labour market at anything other than the level of menial low-paid jobs. Drugs dealing served as a useful alternative. Others though combined their rave drug selling lifestyles alongside professional employment and conventional lives.

A theme that interweaves with drugs dealing as alternate work is borrowed from Ruggiero and South's work (1995, 1997). This takes the notion of 'crime as work', but adds an analysis of the urban city environment. They note that with a large population size, and transient and anonymous make-up, multiple work type opportunities are provided, which span both legal and illegal economic spheres.

This construct is enhanced by earlier works developed within urban sociology on city cultures, specifically the way human relationships and interactions in large urban settings comprise loose social ties due to the size and density of city populations. Relationships in large cities are seen as more functional and anonymous than those of more traditional close-knit communities (Simmel 1903 [2002]; Spykman 1926; Tönnies 1955; Karp *et al.* 1991). There is little more recent literature to draw upon that applies this understanding. Yet, I draw on this and argue the size and nature of the London urban setting greatly facilitated the drug selling set-ups I observed, and sometimes the fleeting, functional and economic relations that underpinned this drugs trade.

Another issue that runs through the stories of the different characters involved in drug using and selling lifestyles is that of shifting and multiple identities, as theorised within understandings of late-modern society (Giddens 1991). Here the notion is that we are no longer bound by fixed identities traditionally linked to social class background, but that we occupy multiple identities shaped through a range of lifestyle choices and options. These different identities are drawn on in diverse contexts and are used to shape our self expression. Many of the people observed in this study came from middle-class social backgrounds, who in addition to living 'deviant' drug-using and selling lifestyles, held conventional jobs and positions of responsibility. In this way they can be seen as oscillating between two identities; occupying a deviant one in one sphere of their lives and a conventional identity in others. Some though were from less advantaged socio-economic backgrounds and the ability to shift identities was a more limited undertaking.

Introductory chapter and book content

This introductory chapter provides the contextual background to the study. A broad overview of the rave club culture since it first emerged in the UK is laid out. The rave club culture underwent a number of transformations and exists in a very different form today to when it first emerged, and indeed to when my field observations were carried out. This is to the extent where it can be questioned whether a rave club culture still exists (Anderson 2009). Nevertheless, a culture of going out clubbing and taking drugs has remained a constant pastime, and continues to underpin the current night-time leisure scenes occurring across city centres in the UK today (Webster *et al.* 2002; Greater London Alcohol and Drug Alliance 2003, 2007). In this way, it can be argued the insights revealed from my field observations in the mid to late 1990s bear resemblance to the drug using scenes occurring today. Also included in this chapter is an overview of the different ways the rave culture has been analysed and understood.

The following chapters are divided up to present a detailed account of drug use and drug selling within the London rave club scene. These involve a broad overview of the London rave club culture at the time my research was carried out with descriptions of some of the venues and social environments my observations were made within (Chapter 2). The drug use styles of the different interlinked friendship networks are described in Chapter 3. Chapters 4 and 5 focus on the organisational features of drug purchasing and selling as it occurred in public nightclub venues and in private social network styles of selling. The safety strategies adopted by sellers in order to avoid being caught are interwoven with the material in these chapters. Chapter 6 examines the role women played in the drug selling process. Women's position within drugs markets are typically depicted as passive yet from my observation of the rave drugs market it was evident that women played active and central roles. They were not often in front-line positions but played important peripheral roles. Chapter 7 discusses the ease with which drug selling set-ups were entered into and scaled-up beyond what people had initially intended. But, the obstacles some of them faced in their attempts to move away from drug selling lifestyles are noted. The concluding chapter looks at the later lives of some of the people written about in the book and summarises the field observations within a framework incorporating notions of illegal enterprise and entrepreneurship, and friendship and functionality in the London urban setting. A brief précis of where we are now in terms of a London rave club drugs culture is also given.

Before moving on, I will clarify some of the terms used within this book in reference to the rave club culture.

Defining the terms

Various terms are used in reference to the rave club culture depending on which era is being written about. 'Rave culture' applied to the period that involved large-scale outdoor rave events (Reynolds 1998), 'ecstasy culture' referred to the widespread

7

diffusion of ecstasy consumption across the young adult population (Collin 1997), and more generic terms such as 'dance culture' and 'dance scene' were introduced in the latter part of the 1990s. These more inclusive terms reflected the expansion of rave culture and the range of venues and contexts in which it was being 'celebrated'.[3] Even more encompassing terms were used to capture its global spread and the associated dance scenes that emerged in different parts of the world. St John (2004) referred to these expanded scenes as 'electronic dance music culture'.

For simplicity, the term used throughout this book is 'rave club culture', though I move back and forth between 'rave club culture' and 'rave club scene'. To some extent, use of the term 'culture' denotes an understanding of it as a defined social and cultural system with codes of practice, rituals and meanings (Geertz 1973). Use of the term 'scene' is illustrative of the broader ambience of rave culture and the way it permeated people's lives and general consciousness.

'Clubbing' and 'partying' are also used interchangeably when referring to the rave club celebration styles. Clubbing relates to earlier styles of celebration where going out to a nightclub was the sole event of the outing. 'Partying' refers to a style of celebration observed later on. This was the extended clubbing excursion which often spanned 24-hour periods and involved visiting a number of venues and locations along the way, such as bars and pubs and peoples' houses, both before and after the club event (*cf.* Malbon 1999; O'Hagan 2004).

The terms 'dealers' and 'sellers' are used when referring to drug sellers. Few people in my study identified themselves as drugs dealers even if they were significantly involved in a drug selling set-up. In respect for the way they perceived themselves, which was generally as *only selling drugs to friends*, in the main I refer to them as 'drug sellers'. The term 'drugs dealers' is used in a more formal sense as I situate my study within a drugs market discourse.

Moving on from the way I refer to the London rave club culture, the following section provides a broad overview of the UK rave club culture. This covers the late 1980s, through the 1990s, to the way this leisure culture can be conceived today. Obviously there were, and still are, numerous types of clubbing style, all with their own unique group affiliations and sets of behaviour (Sanders 2005). These cannot be accounted for in a broad description, yet what is described below encapsulates the defining features and the broad forms the rave club culture took.

The UK rave club culture: an overview

There are varying accounts of the origins of the UK rave club culture. Some place emphasis on the music and club cultures of Detroit and Chicago and the New York 'gay' club scene of the early 1980s (Reynolds 1998). Others focus on the music and party culture that emerged on the Balearic Island, Ibiza (Redhead 1993; Saunders 1995; Shapiro 1999; Van Wijngaart *et al.* 1999). And there is Collin's (1997) journalistic report which pieces together an explanation involving a series of developments occurring from the late 1970s through the 1980s. This included the manufacture of MDMA[4] in pharmaceutical laboratories on the West Coast of the US, and its growth in popularity as a psychotherapeutic aid among what Collins refers to as the 'Californian neuroconsciousness fraternity'. This was before it arrived on the dance floors of nightclubs and began being produced and marketed for recreational purposes (*cf.* Beck and Rosenbaum 1994). Here, it was branded ecstasy and began its diffusion into Europe, commonly suggested via the New Age traveller and hippie cultures living on the Island of Ibiza.[5] In whichever way it arrived in the UK, by the late 1980s the rave club culture had taken off and was drawing in large swathes of young adults across the population, and rave club scenes were becoming established in many cities and towns across the country (Gilman 1991; Merchant and MacDonald 1994; Collin 1997; Reynolds 1998).

Different forms of the UK rave club culture

The UK rave culture can be separated into three distinct phases. The first of these, the early rave culture, was the scene as it first emerged in the mid to late 1980s up to around 1992. The early rave culture stood out mainly for its outdoor existence and the organisation of large-scale illegal rave parties, before newly imposed legislation forced it into licensed leisure venues (Collin 1997; O'Hagan 1999).

The period that followed was from 1992 through to the late 1990s. This period saw the rave club culture diversify into numerous forms, with music genres broadening its appeal to a wide cross-section of people and merging what was previously an underground leisure culture with a more mainstream nightclub scene (Merchant and MacDonald 1994; Thornton 1995; Collin 1997; Reynolds 1998; Malbon 1999). Some analysts observed the early rave culture as largely a white working-class, male manifestation (Thornton 1995), yet as it grew, its membership could no longer be assigned to any

9

one category. Different social classes, men and women, and people from all ages and diverse ethnic backgrounds were involved.

The years of the mid 1990s stood out to be the peak period in the life of the rave club culture. Record numbers were involved and record quantities of drugs were being consumed. Although difficult to quantify, in the year 1993 the Henley Centre for Forecasting documented attendance at British rave club events at over 50 million a year (cited in Thornton 1995). A general estimate was that one million ecstasy pills were being consumed in the UK each week (London Drug Policy Forum 1996). In this way 90s rave club culture became synonymous with illegal drugs culture. Moreover, illegal drug use had permeated British society to such an extent that some commentators argued it could be viewed as a 'normal' part of everyday life. Howard Parker, in developing a sociology of 90s youth, described the drug taking behaviour of UK young people to have become such an unremarkable part of their lives, that it had become a 'normalised' activity (Measham et al. 1994; Parker et al. 1995, 1998). It could be argued that evidence of this drugs normalisation process was, in Britain, being promoted as part of its vibrant and 'cool' youth culture, branding itself 'Cool Britannia'. At this time Britain was being endorsed by both left and right politicians on its powerful youth culture, and the unique club culture and night-time leisure industry was its selling point. Paradoxically, this was a culture whose very existence and success was thriving on a large amount of illegal activity and revenue.

In the latter part of the 1990s and into the new millennium the rave club culture evolved into a different form again. The British Crime Survey – the benchmark of the nation's drug using trends – had implied a plateauing effect in the use of dance drugs (ecstasy, amphetamine and LSD), after the earlier year-on-year increases (Ramsay and Percy 1996; Ramsay and Spiller 1997; Ramsay and Partridge 1999). Yet, rather than plateauing, a different form of drug use emerged. Cocaine made a major appearance on the dance drug stage. Anecdotal reports noted people were switching from using ecstasy to taking cocaine with different styles of socialising accompanying it (Reynolds 1997; Boys et al. 1999, 2002). Various studies have gone on to capture this penchant for cocaine among Britain's young adult population (Ramsay and Partridge 1999; Ramsay et al. 2001; Condon and Smith 2003; Chivite-Mattthews et al. 2005; Hoare 2009; Moskalewicz et al. 2009).

The face of the rave club culture has changed significantly (Anderson 2009), yet there continues to be a considerable number of people who consume ecstasy, cocaine and other drugs in club venues and bars across the UK each week (Webster *et al.* 2002; Greater London Drug and Alcohol Alliance 2003, 2007). This club culture is no longer considered the rave club culture of its traditional form, yet the current form of youth socialising and night-time leisure has its origins in the 80s/90s rave club culture. What has grown out of the rave club culture is a commercialised nightclub cum bar industry, in which leisure entrepreneurs across city centres cater to both the drinking and drug taking styles of today's going-out groups (Carter 2003; Sanders 2005; Silverstone 2005; Measham and Moore 2009). This is alongside freelance leisure entrepreneurs who continue to organise a more underground music and nightclub scene in different venues and spaces around the capital.

In locating the research reported in this book within a particular life stage of the rave club culture, it can be said it was carried out during a period of busy illegal drug using and trading activity, before it evolved into a hybrid drugs and drinking culture.

Rave club culture as a global phenomenon

It is generally accepted that the UK was the front-runner of this unique club drugs culture (St John 2004), and its cultural form was specific to the UK, yet similar styles emerged, and continue to develop in neighbouring European countries, and further afield in Australia, Canada, the United States and many other sites across the globe. To this end, rave club culture can be considered a global phenomenon. Studies carried out in these countries have revealed many similarities to that of the UK in terms of cultural form and drug use patterns (Calafat *et al.* 1998, 2004; Van de Wijngaart 1998, 1999; McElrath and McEvoy 1999; Benschop *et al.* 2002; Korf *et al.* 2003; Engels and ter Bogt 2004; Murphy *et al.* 2005, Hunt *et al.* 2010, among others).

Drugs use among clubbing populations

Through the 1990s different research studies on the nature of drug taking among rave club populations emerged. Most revealed similar findings regardless of which geographical part of the UK the sample was drawn from.[6]

High levels of the use of ecstasy, speed, LSD, cocaine, etc. were recorded (Forsyth 1996a; Branigan *et al.* 1997; Release 1997; Akram and Galt 1999; McElrath and McEvoy 1999; Sherlock and Conner 1999; Hammersley *et al.* 1999, 2002; O'Hagan 1999; Measham *et al.* 2001; Riley *et al.* 2001; Deehan and Saville 2003). Leaving aside cannabis use, ecstasy and speed were typically recorded to be used by 60 to 80 per cent of clubbing samples. Amyl nitrate, LSD and magic mushrooms were usually confirmed as being taken by between 50 and 70 per cent and 'ever use' of cocaine was recorded by 45 to 60 per cent of clubbing populations. The number of people who had tried heroin and crack cocaine was also high (Release 1997; Branigan *et al.* 1997) when compared to general population samples. For example, a survey carried out by Release (1997) recorded that 18 per cent had tried heroin and 18 per cent crack cocaine.

Rave club participants generally distinguished their drug use as recreational and distanced themselves from 'hard-end' drug use styles (Merchant and MacDonald 1994; McElrath and McEvoy 2001), but as the culture developed, anecdotal reports surfaced suggesting people were using heroin to assist the 'come down' from stimulant drugs effects. A small pilot study with young opiate-dependent patients found just over a third (34 per cent) of the group reported their first experience of 'any opiate' was in the context of coming down from ecstasy (Gervin *et al.* 1998). More recent surveys of clubbing populations record lower levels of heroin and crack cocaine trial, such as six and seven per cent respectively in Measham *et al.*'s study (2001), and four and seven per cent in Deehan and Saville's study (2003).

In the later years of the 1990s and into the new millennium cocaine was being used by increasing numbers of rave club participants, compared to earlier on, and this trend was reflected in a number of studies (Winstock *et al.* 2001). Riley *et al.*(2001, 2004) reported from two studies carried out with clubbing populations within two years of each other, that there was a significant shift towards cocaine use. They added that this may have been associated with the older age of the second sample, stating 'greater experience in the dance-drug scene was associated with greater exposure to cocaine' (Riley and Hayward 2004: 256).

It has been suggested that a more expansive list of drugs are now being tried by clubbers than was the case in previous years, with new drugs coming on the market, such as ketamine, GHB, MDMA powder, 2CB, DTB, etc. (Deehan and Saville 2003; Moore and Measham 2008).

Most studies carried out with rave club participants, recorded 'poly' drug use and 'co' drug use to be common. Drug using repertoires were not only found to include a range of drugs, but it was usual for combinations of drugs to be taken on a night out. A 'pick-and-mix' type approach was said to typify rave club drug use with different drugs being used at different time points over the course of an evening out (Parker and Measham 1994; Measham and Moore 2009).

Studies recorded similarities in drug use, but there were also differences. A development within research on clubbing populations was to differentiate the sample by event, or music type. This was in recognition that there were differences in drug use among supporters of certain rave music styles (Deehan and Saville 2003; Riley and Hayward 2004). O'Hagan's research (1999) found drug use across a range of drugs to be higher among attendees of techno-music clubs, compared to attendees of garage-music clubs. And Deehan and Saville (2003) found attendees of a 'gay' club night reported much higher levels of drug use across a variety of drugs, compared to attendees in the other venues.

Rave club drugs health information and education

During its peak in the mid to late 1990s, the rave club culture came under periods of intense media and public criticism. This largely surrounded the widespread drug use that was a part of it, but also the occasional ecstasy-related death. For the most part though it was considered a recreational drug using culture participated in by normal young people who managed their drug using lifestyles alongside their work and home lives. This contrasted with viewing rave clubbers as a group 'whose drug use posed a threat to society's *status quo*' (Akram and Galt 1999: 221).

In the main, dance drug use was viewed as being without the health problems generated through other styles of Class A drug use, such as heroin and crack cocaine. Nonetheless, drugs health professionals voiced concerns at the large numbers of people consuming different stimulant and hallucinogenic drugs and at a frequent rate (Henry 1992; McGuire *et al.* 1994; Thompson 1996; Parrott 2002). In recognition of this as an ongoing and determined drug user population and one defining its drug use as recreational in nature, the need to communicate innovative health education messages was argued (McDermott *et al.* 1992). In the way the drugs 'harm reduction' philosophy had been acknowledged as more beneficial than drugs prevention approaches when working with committed heroin users, transmitting messages of safe club drug use was considered the way forward (McDermott *et al.* 1992; Branigan *et al.* 1997; Measham and Moore 2006).

Cartoon sequences were produced in colourful information pamphlets to express real-life dance drug risks. The most infamous character was 'Peanut Pete' devised by the drugs agency Lifeline in Manchester. Messages conveyed the need to drink water while dancing on ecstasy in hot clubs, taking frequent rests from strenuous dancing to avoid overheating and being aware of who you purchased your drugs from.

It took time for the government of the day to acknowledge the magnitude and reality of this drugs culture (Measham and Moore 2006), and strenuous efforts by lobbyists to health officials led to the backing of the national Safer Dancing campaign (London Drugs Policy Forum 1996). This illustrated the government's eventual acceptance that targeted drugs harm reduction messages were needed. And the campaign went on to put necessary pressure on nightclub entrepreneurs to give water free of charge to clubbers who requested it (Webster *et al.* 2002).

In light of the perceived decline in the rave club drugs culture, these health information campaigns are no longer prominent, yet increasing attention is being directed at recreational cocaine using cultures and the health problems emerging alongside them (The National Treatment Agency for Substance Misuse 2009).

The following section focuses on some specific pieces of work which reveal detail on the internal workings of the rave club drugs market.

Rave club drugs markets

Few studies have examined the organisation of the rave club drugs market in the way that studies of crack cocaine and heroin sellers have done, although there is some work which is useful for viewing the way the market was organised (Dorn *et al.* 1992; Forsyth 1996a and b; Collin 1997; Ward and Pearson 1997; Parker 2000; Pearson and Hobbs 2001, 2004; Silverstone 2003; Sanders 2005, 2006).

Certainly, the dominant suggestion in the literature on drug supply within the rave club drugs market was that it mainly amounted to 'social selling' and that 'friends' were the main source of supply (Dorn *et al.* 1992; Release 1997; Police Foundation 2000; Pearson and Hobbs 2001). Parker (2000) drew on evidence from a study of young adults participating in the rave club scene, and argued, while anonymous nightclub dealers had a 'real involvement' in the sale of drugs to the 'clubbing' population, the majority were obtaining their drugs 'via friends and friends of friends' (2000: 70).

To some extent my interpretations are in conflict with that asserted by other commentators. What I observed out among networks of rave club participants, was that while the majority of people perceived themselves to be purchasing and selling drugs among 'friends' and known contacts, on closer inspection these were often tenuous relationships, sometimes with people they only vaguely knew.

Friends or otherwise, Pearson and Hobbs (2001) noted how busy and lucrative dealing operations within the rave club drugs market could become established within a matter of months. They referred to a 'modern system of fraternity' as respondents typically described accelerations in selling within explanations of expanding friendship networks and familiarity, as described by this young man:

> It kind of escalates quite easily . . . it gets around that you can sort people out for drugs, and friend of friends . . . that sort of thing . . . You know, then their friends want, and their friends want . . . and friends want, and friends want and eventually you've got other people who want to start dealing and then dealers buy from you, and it's a sky-rocket before you even know it. (Pearson and Hobbs 2001: 32; *cf.* Pearson and Hobbs, 2004)

The majority of drug sellers I came to know were not functioning at the same level as the sellers in the Pearson and Hobbs study, though the same acceleration in selling operations was observed. Friends, and friends of friends, attempted to access drugs from one another and anyone they met who was selling them.

There is some work that investigates the nightclub as a drugs marketplace (Morris 1998; Silverstone 2003; Sanders 2005), though detail surrounding 'club floor' drug selling operations remains relatively sparse (Pearson 2007). One study focusing on the nightclub as a drugs marketplace was that by Morris (1998). He focused on the role of nightclub door security in drug selling, and showed how the rave nightclub scene had created a drugs market providing a 'new front' for criminals. Hobbs and colleagues' study (2002) of 'bouncers' and the night-time economy, also noted the lucrative criminal opportunities facilitated through the position of door security personnel.

As the rave club culture developed, media reports emerged claiming door security staff were involved in selling operations inside clubs. It was believed the door security's own contacts were let in, and providing the selling was discreet, a policy of looking the other way was maintained. With this, it appeared some management systems were complicit in the existence of drugs trading in clubs. This was noted by Sanders (2005) from his research carried out as a member of a security team in a London nightclub. He noted that security staff were ideally positioned to be involved in drug sales, and commented on how the official line that drugs in clubs won't be tolerated, 'was a façade', and only served to suggest to the law enforcement authorities that clubs were doing all they could to control drug use within the club (Sanders 2005: 248).

Silverstone (2003) also drew attention to the seemingly relaxed approach to illegal drug activity within the nightclub leisure culture. He theorised what was occurring in respect to the rave club drugs culture as connected to historical developments, such as the way, over time, previous illegal behaviours had become tolerated and legalised.[7] He discussed the historical separation of public and private space and stated there had been 'an expansion in tolerance to acts that occurred in private' (Silverstone 2003: 211). To Silverstone nightclubs were an example of this expansion.

My study sheds light on this in its illustration of nightclub based drug selling that was tied up with management systems.

Theorisations of rave club culture

Rave club participation: protesters and entrepreneurs

Various theoretical studies have examined aspects of the rave club culture such as the meaning and significance it played in the lives of those involved.

These started out with structuralist interpretations that linked it to the 80s 'Thatcherite' political and economic period in which it emerged. The unique conditions established at this time were viewed as providing a suitable environment for the rave culture to surface. The way rave culture was being expressed through the organisation of large-scale illegal raves and widespread drugs use was believed to signify a collective response to the way young people in particular were experiencing 'Thatcher's Britain'. These activities were seen as a form of protest and as symbolising dissatisfaction with the political system (Redhead 1993; Collin 1997; Rietveld 1998b; Wright 1998).

But the dual side of 'Thatcherism', such as the individualist entrepreneurial spirit, and the promotion of a business culture, was also seen to be relevant to explaining aspects of this leisure culture. Some commentators viewed young people's involvement in the commercial aspects of it, regardless of the illegality, such as drugs dealing and the organisation of illegal 'pay parties', to be indicative of the enterprising and self-help attitude valued by Thatcherism. Young people were seen to be appropriating aspects of 'liberal capitalism' for their own ends (Collin 1997; Shapiro 1999). Russell (1993) made this connection. He drew attention to the spirit of self-made entrepreneurship of young people with few alternative opportunities.

> The whole kind of raison d'être of Thatcherism and the political and economic culture was to do it yourself, get off your arse, make some money, get rich quick. For [people] . . . in their teens or their early twenties who didn't have the educational privilege or motivation to do a 9 to 5 straight job, or the opportunity to do it, or even the inclination to want to do it . . . the way that they could get rich and make their money was to sell drugs. (Nathan McGough, manager of the Stone Roses, quoted in Russell 1993: 130)

Collin (1997) also made the link between young people's involvement in the income generating opportunities of the rave drugs economy and the new spirit of capitalism promoted through Thatcherite ethics: 'Ecstasy culture provided an outlet for, even amplified, these entrepreneurial impulses; it enabled people to get involved, to do something, whether it be making a record or selling a bag of pills' (1997: 7).

The view of rave club entrepreneurialism was expanded out from drug selling to include an account of the way young people were engaged in shaping the broader culture and economy of which they were a part. Smith and Maughan (1998) noted a range of areas within the rave club culture where young people could be seen as active economic agents, such as in their involvement in club night and dance party organisation, art working, setting up record labels, running specialist record shops and becoming DJs. To Smith and Maughan, young people were playing an important role in the production of the culture. They stated:

There is an identifiable group of young people working within the cultural sphere who are actively engaged in transforming the structure, not only of contemporary culture, but also of the economic organization of that culture. Young people therefore should not be seen as a group that threatens the social order and needs to be 'dealt with' . . . but as individuals and members of collectives which are at the forefront of creating a new culture and economy. (Smith and Maughan 1998: 212)

So, whereas some social and cultural theorists viewed rave club participation as an expression of protest, others introduced ideas of entrepreneurship. The subject of entrepreneurship and enterprise is a key a theme within this book. The stories that are laid out in the following chapters illustrate the varied innovative ways in which rave club participants employed their entrepreneurial acumen and capitalised on the legal and illegal economic opportunities available within this leisure culture.

A key characteristic of the UK rave club culture was its ability to draw in people from different social backgrounds, but this social pluralism was at odds with dominant hypotheses of UK youth cultural theorising up to that point. Up to the late 1980s, youth cultural theory had drawn on 'subcultural' and 'deviance' theory developed through the University of Birmingham's Centre for Contemporary Cultural Studies (CCCS). Youth cultural expression, which included illegal drugs use, was seen as linked to issues of social class distinction; urban deprivation and social dislocation (see Hall and Jefferson 1976). The general consensus within 90s youth sociology, however, was that the application of subcultural and deviance theories was redundant in light of the socially diverse membership of the rave club culture (Melechi 1993; Merchant and MacDonald 1994; McRobbie 1994).

UK drugs culture and late-modern society

As the rave club drugs culture increasingly merged with mainstream youth culture, and notions of deviance were seen as outdated, conceptualisations became underpinned by understandings of the way the changing social and economic structures of late-modern society[8] were impacting on youth and drugs cultures. This included changes that were occurring to our sense of 'self' and self-identity

(Parker *et al.* 1995, 1998; Malbon 1998, 1999; Bennett 1999; Muggleton and Weinzierl 2003; Hayward 2004).

For instance, Parker *et al.* (1995) drew on conceptions of changing society as assisting to form the unique drugs culture we were seeing in the UK. This was in the way we had seen a reshaping of class and gender relations, which they noted was evident in the changed drug use patterns. Being female and middle class no longer prevented a person from drug use, as numerous social surveys were confirming. Another area of social change Parker and colleagues noted to be impacting upon, not only rave drugs culture but also the broader drug use culture that had developed in the UK, was the forces of globalisation and free-market economics. For Parker *et al.* the wide availability and cultural acceptability of drugs was indicative of advancements in telecommunications and transportations which assist drug supply systems to develop and penetrate. Another area was in the way illicit drugs culture had become integrated into contemporary youth culture. Parker *et al.* saw the blending between drugs culture and more general youth culture as illustrated in the way youth magazines, music, advertising, marketing and fashion and popular language, were appropriating imagery and aspects of rave drugs culture.

Rave club participation: contemporary youth sociality

In light of the mismatch between traditional subcultural and deviance theories and the youth cultural forms of the 1990s and the new millennium, another literature emerged.

A theme filtering through sociological discourses in the early years of the new millennium was that the range of youth cultural groups, whose ways of being centred on music and style, were bound up within conceptions of late-modernity and changing forms of self-identity and self expression. This conceptualisation formed the underlying premise of what was referred to as 'post-subcultural' theorising (Bennett 1999; Muggleton and Weinzierl 2003). A central hypothesis of late-modernity is that individuals' personal identities are 'fluid' and that group identity and cultural belonging is less linked to our social class backgrounds than it was in a previous period. People are viewed as being able to shape their identities through a range of lifestyle choices and options (Giddens 1991). Here then, the view is that we live within a state of multiple identities that can be shaped depending on how we wish to present ourselves. With this it is assumed we can attach ourselves to different groups and social scenes in accordance with how we choose to express our self-identity.

Bennett (1999) worked significantly with ideas of contemporary youth sociality, self identity and self-expression and connected it to notions of lifestyle choice. He discussed rave club participation, but believed his theory applied to the host of identifiable youth cultures that emerged in the UK in the post-war period. Bennett argued the social groupings of contemporary youth were 'examples of late-modern lifestyles in which notions of identity were "constructed" rather than "given", and "fluid" rather than "fixed"' (1999: 599). According to Bennett, what we were seeing within the 'urban club scene' was an example of a form of late-modern sociality whereby people moved between different groups, adopting different identities and personas depending on how the mood took them. The notion of fluid and multiple identities is applicable to the stories that are told in the following chapters in the way people moved between so-called deviant identities in their drug using and drug selling lives, and their more conventional professional and work oriented lives.

Rave club 'togetherness', belonging and community

The significance of the sense of belonging and sense of community that could be achieved through membership in the rave club culture was highlighted in various enquiries (Pini 2001; Gauthier 2004; Olaveson 2004). One interpretation embracing understandings of belonging was that developed by Malbon, published in *Clubbing: Dancing, Ecstasy and Vitality* (1999). His work was centrally concerned with the *experience* of clubbing, which he unravelled through an intricate analysis of 'the night out'. He pointed to the sense of identity and belonging a person could draw through the club night experience. This included the influence of the music and the drug experience. He proposed the notion that when we came together in a group situation we often felt: 'as though we have temporarily lost our individual identities and are instead part of a collective subject' (1998: 277).

Some commentators likened the sense of togetherness and belonging experienced through membership in the rave club culture to that achieved through allegiance to a religion (O'Hagan 2004; Olaveson 2004; Gauthier 2004). This was approached from a similar angle to that applied by Malbon (1999) in that the whole experience of rave club membership was embraced, including the sense of togetherness that occurred within the walls of clubs. Olaveson (2004) wrote about the embodied place the rave club experience took you to, which could be equated to the same connectedness and *communitas* achieved through religious affiliation. He stated 'scholars have begun to conceptualise raving as a transformational and spiritual practice, raising the possibility of viewing rave as a new religious movement' (2004: 85). O'Hagan (2004) made parallels with the UK garage-music scene and gospel-music traditions. He stated they followed 'the same ritualized procedures of interaction, which foster a sense of belonging and communion . . .' (2004: 191).

The sense of togetherness and belonging attained through participation in the London rave club culture was an important aspect for the people I observed and socialised among, and as I will go on to point out this group camaraderie was a key facilitator in the expansion of the drug selling operations I observed.

Rave club participation: status and 'subcultural capital'

A different use of subcultural theorising was prsented in Thornton's explanation of rave club participation, published in *'Club Cultures'* (1995). Emerging from an ethnographic analysis carried out in the early years of the UK rave culture, a key concept she developed was the notion of 'subcultural capital'. This built up from the work of Bourdieu (1984). Bourdieu's work discussed the way in which cultural, social and economic capital translated into social standing. Thornton added 'subcultural capital' to this. She conceived of 'hipness' as a form of 'subcultural capital', and in the same way these other forms of capital could benefit a person's social standing, so too did 'hipness'. Thornton describes how 'DJs, club organisers, clothes designers, music and style journalists and various record industry professionals' could all make a living and enjoyed a lot of respect because of their high volume of subcultural capital (1995: 12).

The concept of subcultural capital has relevance to my research in that it is useful for understanding how people gained credibility, recognition and status from the roles they played as drug sellers within this leisure culture.

In addition, drug using within this culture was analysed within discourses of pleasure (Hunt and Evans 2008; Hunt *et al.* 2010).

What has been laid out above is a broad account of the different ways the UK rave club culture has been theorised. Some of this has direct applicability to the way I consider the drug selling activities observed through my study into this leisure culture.

The following section provides an account of how I came to be studying the rave club culture in the first place, and introduces the key characters and friendship groups on whom the stories laid out in the following chapters are based.

My entry into studying the rave club culture

How did I come to be doing a study of this nature in the first place? Following the completion of my undergraduate degree in May 1993, I gained employment in the drugs research field. At the time I was entering this profession the London rave club culture was gaining momentum, and on some fronts raising concerns. There was a great deal of tabloid newspaper reporting on the large numbers of young people attending illegal rave events and the wide-scale ecstasy consumption that was going on as a part of them. The growing diffusion of the rave culture was also evident in the fact that as I went about my everyday business, I was meeting people of all ages who had become involved. It was around this time that I met Colin. He was a keen clubber and drug taker and regularly took ecstasy on his nights out. He was fascinated by the rave club culture, spoke endlessly about it and, on learning of my job as a drugs researcher, was adamant this was a drugs culture that needed researching. He insisted I join him on one of his club outings to see what was going on.

Out of curiosity, I decided to accompany him and over the following weeks I joined him at some of the nightclubs he had been going along to. It was an eye-opening experience. They were full to capacity, a swirl of young men and women high on ecstasy, dancing for hours in trance like states to DJed techno-music. No secret was made of their drug taking, and those selling ecstasy pills in the clubs were doing little to conceal their selling activity. I too was fascinated by what I was seeing and considered this style of drugs consumption, along with the illegal drugs economy that was accompanying it, worthy of a detailed academic investigation.

It was from this brief introduction to the London rave culture by Colin that my research was formalised in a doctoral study and thereafter my nights out clubbing became entwined with an ethnographic enquiry into the drug using and selling lifestyles of what was to become a large overlapping network of young and older participants.

So, my entry into the rave club culture and my consequent study of it was largely through my association with Colin. Colin and I became good friends and in the first year of my field observations we went out on numerous nightclub excursions. He showed me the way in clubs. In them he constantly roamed around chatting to anyone and everyone, locating sellers, discussing their merchandise, making purchases and having a good time.

As the months passed, Colin began socialising in a different branch of the rave club culture, and for the remainder of my fieldwork his social networks were not a central focus of my observations, though Colin remained a vital character and performed a 'key informant' role throughout the duration of my research. He was there from the beginning to the end. Through his ongoing attachment to a rave club lifestyle, he filled important gaps in my knowledge and assisted in interpretations of this drugs culture and economy.

As Colin moved on, there was another key character who similarly played a crucial facilitating role. This was Andy. I was introduced to Andy in December of 1993 by Colin one Friday night in a club in south London. They had just met, in the way Colin regularly engaged total strangers in clubs in conversation, musing about the DJ and the quality of the ecstasy tablets and who in the club might be selling them. In the same way Colin and his friends were attending the south London club each Friday night, so were Andy and his friends. They loved the 'hard' techno-music the DJs played as well as the raw ambience of the club. Andy was completely immersed in the rave club lifestyle. He was 20 and had been going out clubbing since age 17. He was what you would call a 'busy mover'. He used the rave club culture to make friends and make money. Andy bought and sold small amounts of cannabis, ecstasy, speed and LSD, to friends and anyone else he met along the way who wanted them.

It was through these shared clubbing experiences in the south London club that I began hanging around with Andy's group, and later on with other friendship groups Andy linked in with. On top of cultivating his low-level drug selling, Andy mastered skills in techno-music DJing and went on to become a small-time leisure entrepreneur in organising his own well attended club nights. Leisure entrepreneurship of this type had Andy constantly on the go, and constantly gathering new friends. It was through being welcomed into this lively social scene that my movement among a series of friendship networks whose lives were immersed in the

London rave club culture was made possible, and from which the main characters and club venues written about in the following pages emerged.

Over the five years (1993–1998) I hung around in the London rave club culture I got to know large numbers of people in different nightclubs and dance parties, and through various social and friendship networks. There was a large degree of camaraderie in the rave club culture and friends and clubbing companions were easily made. My approach of being out among rave club participants and blending in produced a large network of consistent contacts. If I restrict this to the people who formed the main focus of my enquiry and who either individually, or as a group, informed my investigations, approximately 50 people were involved. Loosely these belonged to five different friendship groups and my story is built up through the interactions of the 'core' and 'peripheral' members of these five groups. Some characters I write about are detached associates, not necessarily connected to a group, but who were met out in the London nightclub terrain and who for a time became linked to network members. This was usually through the role they were playing in selling drugs. The reality of this club drugs culture was that useful contacts were latched onto to assist in securing drug supplies, and this included anonymous sellers in clubs.

From the larger network of 50, I focus on a smaller number of six people. This is connected to their central involvement in selling drugs and their busy, organisational lifestyles provide a focal point for much of the drugs interactions and relationships laid out in the following pages. These are Colin, Andy, Robin, Rex, Joe and Mick. Aside from Colin, all were friendship network drug suppliers and much group activity and communications occurred around them. Since Colin was not a friendship network supplier the discussions through the book are on six key characters but five friendship networks. Going out clubbing was a group activity and the person/s in a friendship network positioned as the group drug supplier was a central contact point in the preparations running up to a night out. This is the role Andy, Robin, Rex, Joe and Mick performed. (All the names of people and venues have been changed to prevent identification.)

It is difficult to write exclusively about the make-up of the different friendship networks. These were fluid social groupings. New recruits to the scene were added, and groups changed in form as people moved on – either to new groups, or away from the rave club scene altogether.

The five different but interconnected friendship networks comprised people from mixed socio-economic backgrounds, ages and ethnicities. This was as much a feature of the heterogeneity of the London population, as it was the nature of the rave club culture. London is a city with a large multicultural, transient population where people come to live and work from different parts of the country and abroad (Benedictus 2005). Social and friendship groupings in London represent this diversity. Rave club friendship groupings were certainly based on authentic kinship and reflected the diverse profile of the London population, but they were also based on a shared sense of purpose in terms of going out clubbing and taking drugs. Thus, a unique feature of this leisure culture was that friendship groups were made up of what might be seen as unlikely alliances of people. There were often wide age gaps between friendship group members and glaring socio-economic differences. It didn't matter. Rave club membership was about going out clubbing, taking drugs and having fun.

The five friendship networks can be viewed as linked in the way that the central characters in the end came to be connected to each other, and the resultant overlap between network members. Drug sellers linked in with each other, both to assist ease of access to drugs and good deals, as well as providing a source of mutual support.

The linking of three of the friendship networks also came about through their regular socialising at a popular, north London DJ bar. This was Robin's, Rex's and Mick's groups and Andy also became a part of this grouping. He was a key link in some of the connections being made as a part of this vibrant party group.

The stories in the following chapters centre on these key people, and on others attached to their groups.

Below the six key characters and their friendship groups are introduced.

Key character introductions

Colin

Colin is a key character in this story of the London rave club culture. He was there from the beginning to the end. In the early stages Colin was linked to Andy's friendship network. This was through spending nights out in the same nightclub together and afterwards at chill-out sessions. As time passed, Colin moved into a different style of rave club socialising and did not become linked to the other five friendship networks whose activities make up this story. Colin was 23 when we met in 1993. He was white, English, well educated and well travelled. He hadn't long lived in London. Before that, he'd been working as a hairdresser in Sydney, Australia. Now he was working as a warehouse manager. He was capable of more, but for the time being he didn't care. He loved going out clubbing and loved taking drugs. The job paid the rent, wasn't too demanding and, importantly, didn't interfere with his clubbing lifestyle. Colin searched London listing magazines, selecting different techno-music club nights to try out. Each week he went along to one, sometimes two. Some of his friends, including his girlfriend, didn't share his enthusiasm. He wasn't bothered. He simply went out alone and latched on to people who did.

Andy

Andy is a key character in this story. Field observations concentrated on Andy's friendship group from the early months of my entry into the London rave club culture, to the end. Over the course of my hanging around with Andy he was aligned to different friendship groups. He moved from one group to another, as new economic opportunities opened up, groups disbanded or changed in form, or as he simply met new people he preferred going out clubbing with. The group I refer to as Andy's group, are the friends he was attached to when I first met him, and with whom he maintained a loyal friendship throughout. These were his long-time male friends from his local area. They were around nine in total.

Andy was 20 when I met him through Colin in the south London club in 1993. He was white and was born and brought up in the suburbs of south London, raised single-handedly by his mother in a household where money was tight and luxuries were scarce. He'd left school at 16, and had since moved in and out of low-paid jobs and claiming benefit. He was a keen club-goer and techno-music enthusiast. Along with his friends he went to numerous club nights in and around London each weekend. He was his group's leader, connected to the central organising role he took in ensuring ecstasy supplies for the group's nights out. Like Andy, all of the group were white, aged 20 and 21, were single and lived at home with their parents. And also like Andy, most were moving back and forth between signing on the dole and in and out of low-paid work. They took ecstasy and speed regularly and smoked cannabis heavily.

Joe

Joe is also a central character in this story whose busy drug selling operation among a large group of free-party people provided fascinating insights into heavy drug using styles and the intricate dynamics of friendship network drug selling. I met Joe through Andy in 1994. Joe and Andy became friends. They were introduced through a mutual friend not long after Andy moved up from the south London suburbs. Joe was 20. He was white, middle class and had been born and raised in north London. He was studying at a reputed London university but was on a year out from his studies so he could enjoy his clubbing lifestyle without the pressures of exams and deadlines. He was not the type you'd associate with drug selling. He was a quiet character, but this was as much a tactic as a feature of his personality. A priority for Joe was drawing as little attention to himself as possible. This wasn't easy. Joe's friendship network was large in number. They totalled around twenty at any given time.

His friendship group were varied in age and social background. Some were in their early 20s, and others were in their 30s. Some were from privileged middle-class backgrounds holding university degrees and professional jobs, and others were employed in manual labour and low-paid work. A few had come to London from different parts of the UK, and a few were from other European countries. The majority of them lived independently in shared housing arrangements and some were in couple relationships. This group was one of high revelry and heavy drug use. They used a wide range of stimulant and hallucinogenic drugs including 'speed', ecstasy, LSD and magic mushrooms, and drank alcohol heavily.

Robin

Robin is also a key character and was a friendship group leader based on her position as a drug seller. I met Robin through Andy three years into my field observations in the late months of 1996. Robin's ongoing drug selling out in public arenas and among an expansive group of clubbers provided particular understandings of the networked reality of this drugs culture and economy. Robin was from Australia. She was aged 21 when we met and was in London on a two-year working holiday visa. She was loud, had a big character, was full of confidence and loved to party. Robin left school with few qualifications, but had gained sought-after office administration skills and during her time in London worked in well-paid jobs in banking institutions. This was alongside selling ecstasy, speed and cannabis to an extended network of fellow Australasians and others. Robin's core friendship group was made up of around fifteen people, and as with all these groups, they were added to by new and changing members. Most were aged in their early 20s. The majority were white and a few were black or mixed-race Londoners. Males and females were equally a part of the group. They were variously employed. Some held professional jobs, and others had employment of a more temporary nature, enabling them to live out their two-year working holiday visas with limited responsibility and maximum freedom. They regularly took ecstasy tablets, speed and sometimes cocaine, and cannabis and alcohol was consumed heavily.

Rex

Rex is another central person in my observations. He became a part of my study at the same time as Robin in the late months of 1996, and was someone on whom my observations were focused for two years. He and his friendship group became subsumed within Robin's. Rex also sold drugs and had for a long time. With this, he knew to keep the focus off himself. He was older and more experienced. He was white and aged 40. He was always just sort of there, on the scene but remaining discrete. Rex helped Robin, in a 'minder' kind of way.

Mick

Mick was also a key character and was a friendship group leader, based on his role as a drug seller. I met Mick early in 1997 when field observations began to coalesce around the activities and interactions of three overlapping friendship groups. These were Robin's, Rex's and Mick's and were connections linked to the social interactions and formations that grew up around a busy north London DJ bar where all three groups regularly socialised.

Mick was white and aged 22. He was originally from the Midlands. He was a popular person, not only based on his drug supply, but on his amiable and caring character. He was surrounded by a close-knit group of solid friends who regularly met up to watch football in local pubs. The broader group numbered between ten and fifteen. This was a mixed group, including Londoners and others living in London from different parts of the UK and abroad. They were aged in their early 20s, with a few close to age 30. They were variously employed, working in bars, as DJs, in club organisation, in the media industry, and a few were on vocational training courses. Some claimed unemployment benefit. A few lived at home with their parent/s. Others lived in shared accommodation with friends. They were regular cannabis smokers and drinkers and were more inclined to use cocaine than ecstasy.

The stories in the following chapters centre on these people, and on others attached to their groups. The key characters were typically the friendship group leaders linked to the role they played in drug selling. Drug sellers were popular people. People congregated around them to ensure ease of access to a supply of ecstasy or cocaine.

Broadly these friendship groups could be located within the techno-music scene of the rave club culture, but clear divisions were difficult to draw. People socialised in all sorts of venues and attached themselves to, and moved between, a number of different friendship groups and scenes, all with slightly different tastes in clubbing, music style and drug taking behaviour. It was not uncommon for people to go to a commercial nightclub in central London one weekend and to a 'squat party'[9] out in the country the next, depending on which friendship group they chose to align themselves to that night.

It must be noted though that it was difficult to locate people precisely in one or other part of the rave club culture. Rave club sociality was fluid in nature with people socialising in different parts of the scene and among different groups, depending on what social group they had become aligned to.

The following chapter describes the venues and social spaces in which my research was carried out.

Notes

1 Through Becker's close associations with marijuana users he revealed that it wasn't simply the effect of the drug, but one had to learn the process of being 'high'. Polsky provides rich detail about the consumption of drugs in the beat scene and the group divisions by different drug preferences.

2 Ethnographic studies which have provided insights into drug dealing include Adler's (1985, 1992) study of upper-level cocaine sellers in California, Waldorf and colleagues' (1991) study providing intricate detail on friendship group cocaine selling in the San Francisco Bay area, Johnson and colleagues' (1985) study of heroin sellers in Brooklyn. Williams (1989) conducted an

extended ethnography among a friendship network of young 'crack' and cocaine users and dealers operating on the Upper West Side of Manhattan, Dunlap and colleagues (1994) studied female crack sellers in Harlem. There is also Jacobs' (1999) study of young crack sellers in Missouri, and Bourgois (1995) went to live in a Puerto Rican neighbourhood on Manhattan's Upper East Side where he immersed himself in the crack cocaine using culture of local residents by living in the area.

3 I sometimes use the term 'celebration' when referring to peoples' involvement and attendance at club events and dance parties. This particular parlance has been chosen because it aptly illustrates the sense of festivity and merriment people displayed in their attachment to these cultural arenas and entertainment sites (Silverstone 2003; Gauthier 2004).

4 Ecstasy was chemically known as MDMA – methylenedioxymethamphetamine 3, 4.

5 There are other accounts of how ecstasy arrived in Europe. For instance, Saunders (1993, 1995) wrote of it being bought to Europe in the mid 1980s by followers of the Rajneesh movement (1993: 17).

6 A range of sampling strategies was used to access club drug users, including research teams basing themselves in nightclubs to question clubbers, readers of dance music magazines being asked to complete questionnaires, and 'snowballing' through participants active in rave club culture.

7 Silverstone included homosexuality and prostitution. Although prostitution in the UK isn't illegal, he contended the existence of 'off-street' sex sites supporting the industry, such as massage parlours, saunas and strip clubs, etc. could be viewed as a partial move towards the tolerance and decriminalisation of this activity (2003).

8 A range of terms are employed in reference to the changing order of society, such as late-modernity, post-modernity, modernity, late-modern society etc. In essence, this is an issue of semantics, incorporating similar notions of cultural, social, technological and economic change (Hayward 2004: 47). For simplicity, through this book the changing social and economic systems we have experienced in the last few decades and the incumbent modifications this has had on our sense of self, identity and expression, are generally referred to as 'late-modern society'.

9 'Squat parties' was the term used for the parties organised by the free-party scene.

Chapter 2

Organisation of the London rave club scene

> Clubs and raves house ad hoc communities with fluid
> boundaries which may come together and dissolve in a single
> summer or endure for a few years. (Thornton 1995: 3)

In this chapter my examination of the London rave club culture
is further set out by describing the locations and social milieux in
which it was situated. Firstly, an overview of rave club culture as it
appeared in London over the period of field observation is provided.
To achieve this, a typology of the main event types that were being
attended by rave club participants at this time is presented. Also,
descriptive accounts of some of the club venues and spaces the
different friendship networks socialised within are given. This
seeks to contextualise the drug using and selling scenes that are
laid out in the following chapters.

The nightclubs and social spaces the different friendship networks
attended, moved between and bought and sold their drugs in,
formed just one part of a much larger celebratory form. Constructing
a definitive account in its entirety is a difficult task given the many
permutations of the rave club culture. These difficulties were noted
by Thornton (1995). She says: '"clubland" as many call it, is a difficult
terrain to map. Club nights continually modify their style, change
their name and move their location. Individual clubbers and ravers
are part of one crowd, then another and then grow out of dancing
altogether' (1995: 98).

It is necessary to make a brief point about rave club music styles in order to further situate the research. At a certain point rave club music fragmented into numerous different sub-genres, and included an array of music types, with different forms of celebration and drug taking attached. Whilst acknowledging the complex study of rave club music genres (Reynolds 1997, 1998; Rietveld 1998a), it is enough for me to refer to it in broad types such as hard-core, techno, garage, etc. (*cf.* O'Hagan 1999, 2004[1]). In the main my field observations were located within the techno-music scene. In using Andy as a lead through the London nightclub terrain, as well as to access different friendship networks, my observations were located largely within the techno branch of the rave club culture. Andy was a techno-music enthusiast and the majority of clubs I attended as a part of his friendship network socialising were techno clubs. The bulk of the people I focused on also identified within this particular music and club style.

Different rave club music styles were linked with particular types of drug use, and techno and hard-core music followings were said to be connected to higher levels of drug use (Reynolds 1998; O'Hagan 1999). In support of this view, it might be considered that the drug using I observed in the clubs I attended and among the people I came to know, may have been a more committed style of use than that found within other rave club music attachments.

Also useful as contextual information for this chapter is the distinction that can be made in the way the rave club leisure sphere was managed and organised. Broadly this can be divided into leisure that was controlled and organised by commercial entrepreneurs and that which was designed and managed by rave club participants themselves (Chatterton and Hollands 2003). Rave club participants were economic actors involved in the production of the culture and economy of which they were a part (Smith and Maughan 1998). This was through both their input in creating club spaces and hosting profitable nightclub events, and their role in stimulating and perpetuating the illegal drugs economy that surrounded this culture. This innovation and enterprise by rave club participants becomes apparent through the stories and scenarios I recount in the following chapters.

London rave club venues and events

The following classification of rave club venues and events is a reflection of the way the culture evolved over time, yet more accurately, the way it reacted to legislative changes that were being made to bring it into line. A number of amendments were made to the legislation during the 1990s in a direct attempt to bring the rave club culture under greater control and surveillance. A clampdown on early rave type events was implemented, which forced promoters to organise events within officially licensed and more closely monitored venues[2] (Collin 1997). Further changes were made later on which put nightclub managers under greater pressure to control the use and distribution of drugs on their premises.[3] Later on again, in recognition that the club drug scene continued to flourish, renewed pressure was placed on the licence holders of clubs and pubs to assist in the battle to contain drug supply.[4]

The main event types that were going on in London at the time of my research were as follows.

Raves

Raves were the early celebratory form of the rave club culture. These were illegal events organised by entrepreneurial individuals with a personal interest in providing parties for like-minded people. Details of events were passed through word-of-mouth and broadcasting over pirate radio stations. Due to their illegality, the exact locations of events were released only hours in advance. Raves were held in rural areas and usually lasted for extended time periods, between twelve and 24 hours. Large numbers of revellers were attracted. The peak estimate was recorded at a party in Castlemorton in 1992, at which 30,000 people were said to have attended (Collin 1997). As events went unpoliced and functioned in advance of the laws set out to restrict them, drug selling and drug taking was rife (Collin 1997). At the time my research got underway in 1993, raves were nearly a thing of the past. In this case, raves were not among the range of places where my fieldwork observations were carried out.

Commercial rave dance nightclubs

Commercial rave nightclubs were the large popular clubs located in central city areas. Following the legislation that brought rave culture in from the outdoors, purpose-built nightclub spaces located

33

in central urban areas were looked to, to cater for the new demand. Leisure venues dotted in and around London turned to the profits that could be yielded through the pockets of the rave dancer. From an organisational perspective, commercial rave nightclubs were managed in the same way to that of the traditional nightclubs or dance halls. The responsibility for the venue lay within the hands of a nightclub manager and a chief aim was getting people through the door. To attract the rave club clientele, people with specialist knowledge of the music and other clubber tastes and preferences were drawn into management structures and played an important role in the marketing of these clubs.

Commercial rave nightclubs were large in person capacity, generally ranging from between 800 to 1,000. Some clubs became dubbed 'super clubs' in that a commercial empire built up around them. Popular nights of the week for socialising such as Thursday, Friday and Saturday nights were full to capacity as line-ups of well known DJs were put together to draw in the crowds. Commercial rave nightclubs advertised widely in the music and popular press. Large amounts of money were made through these clubs, mainly through the expensive entry fees charged.

As the rave club culture expanded and media reports warned that drugs were rife in clubs, local authorities were forced to impose strict guidance on drug dealing. Nightclubs located in high profile areas came under pressure to observe the licensing laws. As a result, such places became less appealing for some as places of celebration and more risk-laden as places to trade drugs.

Small venue nightclubs

The growth of the night-time economy surrounding the rave club culture saw the range of spaces being used as nightclub venues expand. Purpose-built club spaces were being renovated and turned into rave clubs, as were spaces never previously conceived of for dancing, such as the disused spaces beneath London's many railway arches. Small venue nightclubs operated in a similar way to commercial nightclubs but were much smaller in person capacity (around 500 to 600). Generally these were located away from city centres. Owing to their more hidden locations many of these venues went unlicensed and were free to operate in any way they wished.

Small venue nightclubs differed to commercial nightclubs in the way they were organised: the venue space was hired out on a nightly basis. A fixed-rate fee was charged for the night. Friday and Saturday nights were the most popular nights of the week for clubbing. These were the most sought-after nights by those looking to hire, and the most expensive nights by those doing the charging. The person hiring the space – 'the host' – essentially brought along their own club package, which, when put together, formed the basis of a club night. This consisted of the music in the form of the DJ, the crowd in the form of the people they attracted through their own marketing, and the ambience in the form of the way they chose to decorate the club. Hosts also made sure a supply of drugs was available. The entrance fee was set and collected by the host. The owner or leaseholder of the venue was responsible for providing a suitably maintained space, and usually took responsibility for the bar and alcohol sales. They also laid down the basic rules, such as the opening and closing times of the place, ran the cloakroom facility and employed the security staff to the level and strength deemed necessary.

Moving dance parties

Another club style was what I call the moving dance party. In many ways these were a reaction to the increasing regulation and commercialisation of the rave club culture as a whole and the desire by some leisure entrepreneurs to keep it functioning in a more discreet, underground fashion. Broadly, moving dance parties were small-scale, exclusive, one-off events, which generally required purchasing tickets in advance from an allocated ticket outlet. These were organised in a similar way to small venue nightclubs. Party organisers would find a suitable space for hire and set about organising a party. All manner of venue types were used. Moving dance parties were often held in venues tucked away within London's suburban sprawl and sometimes even further field. Moving dance parties were hosted in places far from intended for party purposes, such as in empty country barns, disused cinemas and leisure boats on the River Thames. In some places everything had to be brought along, from the alcohol being sold, to the sound system, and sometimes port-a-loos too.

Attending moving dance parties required having insider knowledge and hearing through the grapevine when the next party was to be held. Ticket availability was open to the public, but publicity was targeted at specific groups. This was by advertising through locations such as independent record stores and certain boutique clothing shops. Due to the intimate nature of these events, moving dance parties drew repeat crowds of overlapping friendship networks. The familiarity between attendees, and the out of the way locations, meant drug taking and selling was an open activity and took place with little concern.

It was never entirely clear how the organisers got away with these parties. They operated under a different licensing format to those held in more commercial venues, if they were even licensed at all. It was my impression that if an entrance fee wasn't collected on the premises, moving dance parties could masquerade as a private party and were therefore not subjected to the same licensing restrictions.

Pre-club DJ bars

Along with the expansion of the nightclub culture and economy was the growth of pre-club DJ bars. These became an important feature of the rave club culture. They functioned in the same way as any other drinking venue, though live DJs were their special attraction. Pre-club DJ bars provided a convenient meeting place prior to going to a club, and post the clubbing event, the morning after. They could also provide a club atmosphere without having to go out to a club. For people not wanting a whole night out, a visit to a DJ bar could satisfy. Licensing of DJ bars fell under the same terms and conditions as any pub or bar, and closed at 11.00 pm. Sometimes late licenses were granted, usually for private parties and special nights such as New Years Eve. As DJ bars increased in popularity, so too did drug taking and selling at them, and many were forced to employ door security staff in the same form as nightclubs, particularly on weekend nights.

Free-parties

Free-parties were the celebratory style of the squatter contingent of the rave club culture. Free, being the essence of these parties, empty spaces in and around London were squatted to hold them. Such spaces included empty industrial buildings, disused pubs and cinemas, and inner-city car parking buildings, which were taken over and colonised until either the police were alerted, or the last people left. Free-parties could and often did span a 24-hour period. Knowledge of them was strictly word of mouth. In a similar way to raves, these parties functioned with no form of security or policing, providing freedom to purchase, sell and consume drugs at will.

Research sites and venues

The following describes in detail the main focal points and venues where the different friendship networks I socialised among hung out, and where field observations were carried out. Descriptions are given on the physical and structural features of the venues and premises, the ambience and music style of the club or venue space, the clientele attending and the drug use and drug selling styles occurring at them. The different friendship groups are linked to the different venues and events described.

Club London: a commercial rave dance nightclub

Table 2.1   Club London: study period and main features

Club/ venue name	Fieldwork observation period	Type of club/ venue	Clientele	Music style and club ambience
Club London	March 1994 to November 1994	Fixed-site commercial rave nightclub	Young mainly white male crowd, aged between 17 and 22	'Hard-core' techno-music, committed clubbers, dress-down practical clothing style, heavy ecstasy users

Club London was one of a handful of large commercial nightclubs operating in the capital. This was a nightclub Andy's early friendship group attended. They liked it for its high calibre techno-music DJs. Club London was not a club for the faint-hearted. It appealed to the hardened clubber. This was a nightclub that attracted serious devotees to the rave club culture. Club crowds could be ranked according to their dedication to the scene and this was a crowd at the far end of the spectrum in terms of commitment. Ecstasy pill consumption among attendees was heavy. It was not uncommon to see drug casualties lying slumped against the walls in Club London, as the night's drug intake had exceeded even the high doses they could tolerate.

Physical description, capacity and clientele

Club London was a large purpose-built nightclub situated on the edge of the south west London suburbs. It was physically located on the lower level of a large enclosed shopping centre. Club London was a nightclub where the management had turned their attention away from their original clientele, to cash in on the high demand for nightclub space from within the rave club culture. Retaining its original features, including the patterned carpet stairway up into the club, Club London opened in the early years of the 1990s.

Club London had a large person capacity, accommodating between 800 and 1,000 people. It was easy to lose your friends in a club of this size and spend the rest of the evening on your own searching for them. As with other commercial nightclubs of this size and status, people from up and down the country, as well as abroad attended. This widespread appeal was assisted by the high profile advertising, in the form of whole page advertisements in the music and popular press and prominent airtime space on commercial radio. The clientele was largely male, white, and located at the lower end of the clubbing age-range, between the ages of 16 and 22 years.

The large space Club London occupied was laid out on one floor though separated into four different rooms hosting different DJs, thereby producing a range of music styles and providing a choice of atmospheres within the club. The main and largest room hosted the most popular DJs, with the lesser-known ones playing in the smaller rooms. One room functioned as a 'chill-out' space,[5] where a more relaxed music style was played. The main dance floor was bordered by a small carpeted area, complete with a few wooden tables and chairs. Along another wall was a long bar with refrigerator units stocked full of the club's own brand bottled water. Whole enterprises grew up around these clubs, which included marketing their own water. Alcoholic drinks were for sale, but few of the Club London crowd drank alcohol. A common belief at this point in the life of the rave club culture, was that alcohol destroyed the effects of ecstasy. Instead, people drank water, but Club London charged heavily for it (cf. Bellos 1995). To get around paying £1.50 for a small bottle, it was usual for clubbers to buy a bottle on arrival and for the remainder of the evening, fill it from the taps in the toilets. Some nightclubs were unscrupulous with the supply of water on their premises. Club London was one. Filling water bottles from the toilet taps was frowned upon and was even made difficult by the toilet attendant stationed in there to deter people from doing it. No water sales as well as no alcohol sales, was not what commercial enterprise stood for.

Entry to Club London was £12, which was on a par with other commercial nightclubs in London at the time, but was more expensive than many others. These prices were justified by the reputed music DJs booked to play and the club's longer opening hours. Club London closed at 5.00 am, which at this stage was a much later closing time than other clubs. Twelve pounds for seven hours entertainment was considered good value.

Drug selling and security

Commercial nightclubs were prone to more stringent surveillance operations than smaller ones located in less visible parts of the city. Because of this, Club London operated a tight door security system. Everybody but in particular males were searched on entry. However, it was widely accepted that drugs were a necessary ingredient to the success of a club night (cf. Silverstone 2003; Sanders 2005). Even if the management appeared to be observing the law surrounding drug possession and consumption on their premises, a blind eye was often being turned. A number of ecstasy tablet sellers were in Club London selling their supplies. Club London was managed by commercial leisure entrepreneurs and in the thirst for profit, rules were flouted, and safety and welfare were often overlooked.

Lush: a small venue club night

Table 2.2 Lush study period and main features

Club/ venue name	Fieldwork observation period	Type of club/ venue	Clientele	Music style and club ambience
Lush	October 1993 to July 1994	Fixed-site hidden location venue	Young mainly white male crowd, aged late teens to early twenties	Techno-music, committed clubbers, dress-down practical style, heavy ecstasy users

Lush was a small venue club night. This was the south London nightclub where Colin and I met Andy and his early friendship group. In the same way as Colin and I were attending the club every Friday night, so were Andy and his friends. Lush was also not a club for the faint-hearted. This was both in terms of the music played and the no-frills conditions inside the club. As noted, the format of small venue club nights was such that someone hosted the night and the overall organisation and ambience of it was down to them. Lush was hosted by a highly regarded techno DJ, who took audio and visual display to another realm. There were sometimes bizarre live stage shows to accompany the music. One night in the middle of the host's brilliantly crafted, banging techno DJ set, four adults dressed in full body bunny rabbit costumes bounced onto the stage firing blanks into the air from machine guns. It was utter lunacy, but this was part of the uniqueness and appeal of the club. Lush attracted committed techno enthusiasts and as with the Club London crowd, attendees were heavy ecstasy users.

Physical description, capacity and clientele

Lush, was held on Friday nights in little more than an empty space beneath a series of railway arches in a semi-run-down area of south east London. In the early months of its use as a nightclub, the space resembled little more than a cold dank room, with toilet cubicles built into one corner, a makeshift bar along a side wall and a small room at the back of the club. This functioned as the cloakroom. The cloakroom doubled up as a drug selling point. Plastic tables and chairs formed the main seating arrangement, though as the club became more popular, the luxury of seating was dispensed with. Over the months, more investment was put in and the space began to more resemble a nightclub interior.

The venue itself was managed by a south London family. The father was assisted in running the club by his two sons and friends of his sons. These were aged in their early 20s and were variously involved, from manning the cloakroom to selling drugs. Lush had a person capacity of between 500 and 600 and, on most nights, people were turned away. Attendance was 95 per cent male, but as its reputation spread, more women clubbers came along. The majority of attendees was white, aged between 18 and 25 years and typically came from the local south east London area and outlying London suburbs. A range of occupations was represented, such as warehouse storemen, students, record store assistants, and a financial city worker – Phil

– was there most weeks. Occasionally the profile of the crowd changed depending on which DJ had been invited to play. One DJ from Scotland attracted his own loyal following who arrived en masse by coach to support their homegrown talent.

Lush opened at ten at night and closed at 2.30 in the morning, which in comparison to nightclubs opening up in the capital in the years to follow was early. As the nightclub industry expanded, later and later openings were negotiated, with clubs commonly closing at five and six in the morning. Lush operated a membership system. A membership system created a sense of loyalty and helped to guarantee the club a regular audience. Importantly, it was one way of concealing the club's existence and keeping the drug selling operation going on within its walls hidden. Drug selling in clubs was rife, but this was one where the management was associated with it and the least attention drawn to the venue the better.

The dress code for Lush was dress down rather than up. The non-existent heating and ventilation system, in combination with the cold, dank conditions of a disused Victorian railway arch meant a sweater was necessary until a warmth had been created. This was through the sheer body heat created by a mass of people crammed into a small space. From that point on, the ceiling dripped as the moisture produced from hot sweaty bodies collected and rained down from above. At the end of the night when the lights came up, shoes and trouser leg bottoms looked as if they had been tramping through muddy fields and the floor of the club looked like the muddy field.

Drug selling and security

Lush operated strict rules around drugs dealing on the premises. This though was more a concern with their own loss of revenue than for the health and safety of the crowd. Bringing drugs in for personal consumption was acceptable, as long as it was only for personal consumption. Bringing supplies in to sell on to others was strictly forbidden. The drug selling in Lush was in the hands of Ronnie and Vince, who were friends of the owner's sons.

The presence of security staff in Lush was minimal. Safety was not a prime concern, giving the impression that the only role for the security was making sure no one sold drugs on their territory. It was the case that club venues organised in the more 'underground' sphere of the rave scene were less supervised in terms of crowd safety. Lush was no exception. If you glanced around the person-packed space, it was difficult not to feel anxious that in the event of a quick exit being necessary, the sheer volume of people and the limited exits would simply not enable it.

This was a branch of the rave club culture and economy being organised by participants themselves. Where commercial nightclub organisation like Club London was in the hands of commercial leisure entrepreneurs, small venue nightclub organisation was being managed by rave club members. Club organisation like this considered itself more authentic than that managed by commercial leisure entrepreneurs, and clubbers who socialised in this underground club scene distinguished themselves from those socialising in the mainstream commercial sector. The mainstream sector were seen as less immersed in the culture, simply relying on prominent advertising rather than a unique insider knowledge of venues and events.

Tylers: a small venue club night

Table 2.3 Tylers parties study period and main features

Club/ venue name	Fieldwork observation period	Type of club/ venue	Clientele	Music style and club ambience
Tylers	December 1994 to May 1996	Moving-site hidden location parties	Mid-20s, mainly white, employed, male/female crowd	Hard-house and techno-music, sophisticated, dressed-up crowd, keen ecstasy and alcohol users

Tylers was another small venue club night where my observations were made between the end of 1994 and 1996. These were not weekly events. They were held on a random basis, usually about once a month. On most occasions they occupied the same venue but sometimes alternative places were used. Tylers events were attended by different formations of Andy's early group. Andy maintained close ties with his south London friendship group, but he also moved between different groups gathering together anyone who was willing to join him on his nights out clubbing.

Physical description, capacity and clientele

The regular venue Tylers occupied was in a kind of no-man's-land behind one of London's mainline railway stations. This was home to another large capacity and popular nightclub, thereby turning the entire area on Friday and Saturday nights into one of high revelry. The Tylers venue occupied a series of converted railway arches. Disused railway arches became popular as nightclub venues. In contrast to the Lush railway arch venue, a lot of money had been poured into the Tylers conversion. An appealing and tasteful nightclub décor adorned the club space.

As described, the format of small venue club nights was such that someone hosted the night and its overall organisation was down to them. The Tylers hosts were a professional couple aged in their mid-30s and one appeal of their parties was the US techno DJs they booked to play. These were the DJs techno-music fans idolised and at Tylers there was always a group of young men congregating around the DJ booth to get as close to their music idols as possible.

Tylers parties had a mature feel to them. This was in part down to being a Sunday night club. Sunday night clubs had a different ambience. With the next day a workday, some people attended just for a few drinks and to listen to the DJs. But equally there were people there for the full club drug experience. Tylers parties were also hosted on special calendar dates such as Boxing Day night or on Bank Holiday Sundays. These nights had a special atmosphere again. The Tylers crowd was an older group. People were aged in their mid to late 20s, were a balance of men and women and tended towards a more moneyed clientele. The usual venue space hosting the Tylers parties accommodated around 450 people, though depending on whether it was a normal Sunday night or a Bank Holiday Sunday, varying sized crowds attended.

Drug selling and security

The Tylers venue was a registered nightclub space and employed security staff on the door. Although the security guards paid attention to drug possession, people were not rigorously checked. Part of the organisation of small venue club nights was that hosts often took care to make sure a seller would be on the premises to cater for the crowd's drug needs. Whether the Tylers organisers had been active in arranging this was not apparent, but a few people had realised it to be a lucrative selling space and were there on each and every club night selling their ecstasy supplies.

Like the Lush club nights, Tylers nights had an intimate vibe. The Tylers style of club night organisation was also an example of the way entrepreneurial rave club participants identified openings in this leisure market and set about establishing a foothold within it. Tylers provided an example of rave club leisure entrepreneurs with a desire to keep club night organisation in the more underground scene.

Venus Group parties: a moving dance party organisation

Table 2.4 Venus Group parties study period and main features

Club/ venue name	Fieldwork observation period	Type of club/ venue	Clientele	Music style and club ambience
Venus Group parties	August 1996 to December 1998	Moving-site hidden location parties	Mid to late 20s/ early 30s, mainly employed, male/female cosmopolitan crowd	Hard-house and techno-music, sophisticated, fashionable party crowd, keen ecstasy, cocaine and alcohol users

Venus Group events were a series of moving dance parties organised by two friends aged in their early 30s. The Venus Group parties can be viewed alongside the Pace Bar described below. One of the organisers of the Venus Group parties – Tom – was also an owner of the Pace Bar, and many of those who drank in the bar also attended their dance parties.

It was through my regular attendance at Venus Group parties and my frequenting of the Pace Bar through 1997 and 1998 that I came to know the key characters Robin, Rex and Mick, and their wider friendship networks. They all socialised at Venus Group parties and at the Pace Bar. Many of my observations of the drug selling set-ups they were involved in, and the nuanced activity surrounding their drug services, were made among the gatherings in these celebratory spaces. It was also surrounding this vibrant party scene that these friend networks merged into one big one and Andy also came to be a central part of this social scene.

Organisational description, capacity and clientele

Latching on to the financial opportunities being generated through the diversifying rave club culture, the Venus Group set themselves up as organisers of moving dance parties. From a business standpoint, setting up was straightforward. All that was required was to select a trading name and begin trading. In this context, trading meant organising large parties and charging a fee for people to attend. No registration of the company was required, and to keep it simple, payments at all levels of the operation were made in cash. Having a trading name distinguished the party group from similar operations running in the capital at the same time. In addition it provided a name upon which the parties could be marketed to customers.

Surrounding a Venus Group event, the organisational team of two expanded to involve a group numbering between ten and fifteen, sometimes more, depending on the size of the event. This included friends, girlfriends and other more task-oriented assistants such as prop-makers, sound technicians, and general dogsbodies who were useful for transporting and carrying fixtures and fittings along to the chosen venue.

Venus Group events resembled nightclub nights in many ways, though they were organised in an entirely different manner. They were held in clandestine venues in and around London and had an elite feel. Much time would be spent by Tom and his business partner locating suitable spaces for the parties. High levels of secrecy surrounded them. Location details were not revealed until a few hours before the party. This was done through a phoneline being set up with a recorded message giving out details of the party's whereabouts. This helped to avoid detection from the police and licensing authorities. It was also to avoid other party organisers hearing about the same venue space and slipping in before them. Suitable venues became highly sought after, and in the event of another party group slipping in, no protection from the authorities could be called upon.

Tickets were usually priced between £12 and £15 though special occasion events commanded £20 and upwards. This immediately restricted attendance to a more moneyed crowd. Ticket prices were just one expense of a night out. Drugs, alcohol and taxi fares home needed to be included. Typically Venus Group events lasted through the night to the following day, with the party beginning at 10.00 pm and finishing at 6.00 am. At the height of their popularity Venus Group parties were held every few months and were generally organised to coincide with special calendar celebrations, such as Halloween, Valentine's Day and Midsummer's Night. Choosing calendar celebrations meant an automatic theme was given to the party, and the venue space was decorated along the lines of the theme.

Venus group events attracted people ranging in age from their early 20s to their early 30s and were split evenly along gender lines. In contrast to Lush, a 'dress-up' code was adhered to. Women wore skimpy tops and high heels, yet this style was often undermined by the length of the events and the activities going on at them. Many of those adhering to the dress up code looked far from dressed up by the end of the night.

Drug selling and security

Drug purchasing and selling at Venus Group parties resembled a free-for-all. Drug seller territorial rules didn't exist. No person searches were conducted on arrival and although security staff were employed, little if any attention was paid to drug taking or selling at these venues. As long as there were drugs available, the organisers didn't mind who provided them. This again links to the fact that the success of a club night was connected to a general acceptance of drug use and low-level trading. Knowing they were safe zones for selling, a number of people took the opportunity to sell at them. In comparison to other nightclubs, drugs were openly consumed. Cocaine would be sniffed off any dry surface and cannabis 'spliffs' were rolled and smoked wherever anybody wanted.

An example of a Venus Group party

One Venus Group party in February of 1998 was held in a large warehouse in north west London. The venue was a typical industrial style building constructed out of corrugated iron, and was little more than four walls with a roof and a concrete floor. The venue was decorated in true Venus Group style. Elaborate props and soft furnishings were created off-site and carried along and installed at the venue.

The space was actually two rooms. One was the main dance and music room. In the main dance room, the same wooden and metal structures used in stage construction had been erected to create an elevated DJ station and to accommodate the highly expensive sound system. The other room was a more mellow space comprising a calmer music style, a chill-out area and a makeshift bar. The bar was simply a table separating customers from the boxes of beer, cider and vodka-based cocktails being sold.

There were about 400 people at this party, with the usual rituals of drug use and drug selling going on. The party finished around 6.00 am, when the then dishevelled crowd gathered together in groups to make their way home, or to descend on the homes of whoever had offered their place for the 'after party' session. Some joined together and made the quarter-mile walk to the nearest underground station. It was safety in numbers in these circumstances. The world outside the walls of a nightclub was uncomfortable in the drug worn and hungover state most of these partygoers were in.

The Pace Bar: a pre-club/DJ bar

Table 2.5 The Pace Bar study period and main features

Club/ venue name	Fieldwork observation period	Type of club/ venue	Clientele	Music style and club/bar ambience
Pace Bar	August 1996 to December 1998	Fixed-site DJ bar	Mid to late 20s/early 30s, mixed ethnicity in a London way, employed male/female crowd	Hard-house and lounge music, busy and popular meeting place, fashionable rave music venue, mainly alcohol and some cocaine consumption

Pre-club DJ bars became an important feature of the rave club culture. The Pace Bar was one such place. As mentioned the Pace Bar can be viewed alongside the Venus Group events. The Pace Bar opened in late 1996 and before long it was a busy and popular rave club meeting place. Three of the five different friendship groups written about in this book met each other through the Pace Bar and many of the drugs purchase and exchange opportunities were established around them.

Physical description, capacity and clientele

The Pace Bar was located in a busy shopping and tourist area to the north of central London. A regular clientele gathered there on most nights of the week. A friendly and familiar atmosphere grew up around the Pace Bar. People treated it in a similar way to a local pub, dropping in on their way home from work to catch up with whoever of the regulars might be there. Even if no one familiar was there, there was always the DJ to listen to and other people to talk to. There was a strong sense of camaraderie among rave club participants.

The Pace Bar was small in size, though along with its colourful and stylish interior it was designed to maximise people space. This was important. On Friday and Saturday nights hoards of people crammed in to enjoy the party atmosphere. Friday and Saturday nights were the most popular, though DJs were scheduled to play each night of the week, and there were Saturday and Sunday daytime slots as well. More mellow music was played earlier in the week with the tempo building up to a crescendo at the weekend when it resembled a mini nightclub. The Pace Bar functioned as a handy meeting place for people prior to heading out to a club. Besides this, it was a convenient place for people to purchase and exchange their drugs prior to going clubbing. The Pace Bar was also popular with people who weren't in the mood for a whole night's clubbing but wanted something of a party atmosphere.

Drug selling and security

As with any venue associated with the rave club culture, the Pace Bar came to be a place of drug use. The toilets located in the basement were frequently used for sniffing cocaine. This was evident in the pairs of men and women emerging from the cubicles together. Two people in a toilet cubicle was strong indication of cocaine sniffing and was a practice both security personnel and toilet attendants looked out for. As the Pace Bar's popularity increased, it became necessary to employ door security staff to control the numbers entering and to oversee any trouble should it arise, especially on weekend nights. This included keeping an eye on the drug taking on the premises. At a certain stage in the existence of the rave club culture, it was realised that pre-club bars and pubs were also places of drug use and exchange, and these too were drawn into the wider surveillance and control of the scene.

Pre-club DJ bars were also examples of the way the rave club leisure culture was a burgeoning industry. DJ bars were set up by entrepreneurial rave participants as openings in the leisure market were identified for this style of place. Thus, the Pace Bar was another example of the way leisure cultural entrepreneurialism was unfolding as a part of this culture. Some of it was being organised within the underground, informal economy such as Lush club nights, but also legitimate enterprises were being established even if they were buoyed up by a voracious illegal drugs culture. In this way it can be argued that rave club participants were key contributors in shaping the night-time leisure scene that was emerging across the London cityscape at this time.

Thrash parties: a free-party group

Table 2.6   Thrash parties study period and main features

Club/ venue name	Fieldwork observation period	Type of club/ venue	Clientele	Music style and club ambience
Thrash parties	April 1995 to August 1997	Moving-site hidden location parties	Early 20s through to late 30s, mainly white, male/female, 'squatting' scene	Hard-core techno-music, dress down style, excessive ecstasy, LSD, 'base speed'[6] and alcohol use

Thrash parties were another place field observations were carried out and it was at the Thrash parties where Joe's friendship group socialised. These parties were organised by members of the free-party scene. Most of my knowledge of how they were organised, what shape they took, and the goings-on at them, came about through associations with Joe's group. Joe's group was entrenched within this branch of the rave club culture and attended various forms of free-parties most weekends.

The free-party scene was a leisure culture in itself, driven by an ideology of non-conformity and protest, and bound up with a keen enthusiasm for partying and drug taking. People displayed different degrees of commitment to its political, anti-capitalist stance. Some factions were involved in the organisation of high-profile street demonstrations and direct action. Squatting houses and industrial premises to hold parties was another way of expressing their protest. The free-party scene was made up of a number of smaller party groups, all with their own followings. The Thrash party group was one, though the free-party scene identified as one big collective enterprise. Amassing support in large numbers for political protests and street demonstrations was part of the act, as was filling the industrial-sized party venues they regularly managed to squat.

Organisational description, capacity and clientele

Similar to the Venus Group events, rather than occupying one site, these parties were hosted in a range of venues and locations both indoor and outdoor, and in and out of London. Thrash parties were even known to take place in forest clearings and fields out in the countryside. Sometimes smaller groups travelled *en masse* to parties as far away as France and Germany. Here other European free-party groups were joined with. This was a highly transient and mixed group of revellers.

Thrash parties were held on a regular basis, but depended more on whether there had been success with squatting a venue rather than following any formula. A sound system was literally carried along, with any number of hard-core DJs playing over the course of the party. With no entry fee being collected, very little expenditure was put into these events. Occasionally someone paid attention to detail and hung a piece of fluorescent painted fabric in a corner, but generally it was the decaying infrastructure of the building that formed the décor. There were usually limited electrics available in the buildings they partied in, though rigging up a generator to provide a power supply took care of that. Overall, these places were health and safety hazards. If anything did go wrong people would have struggled to get out of some of the places they partied in.

Knowledge of Thrash parties came via the grapevine. In order to avoid police detection, it was necessary to keep details of these parties secret until the last moments before they got underway.

Numbers in attendance depended on the venue and how far the grapevine had reached. The dress code was certainly not a dress-up one. It was more like preparing for an outdoor excursion. Warm clothing was essential for these events even if it was an indoor one. Venues were cold, if not freezing, and with the propensity for parties to last days rather than hours, a warm coat was a necessity. At some stage in the party duration, the coat could double up as a blanket if required. Given the out of the way locations of these parties and the advanced state of inebriation people got into, there was no such thing as going home when you had had enough. You were simply there for the duration and comatose bodies bedded down under coats was not an uncommon sight. Heavy boots also formed part of the uniform. These helped keep out the cold and certainly helped if tramping through fields and mud was involved.

Drug selling and security

The music style at Thrash parties was 'hard-core techno'. This extreme music style coincided with the extent to which drugs were consumed at them. These events functioned with no form of security or policing, providing freedom to purchase, sell and consume drugs at will. Alcohol was popular among this group but it was essential to take your own along. A supply, usually consisting of high-strength cider was sometimes for sale from improvised bars, though this was just a few people serving plastic cupfuls from litre bottles rather than an organised commercial sales point.

An example of a Thrash Party

One Thrash party in the late summer of 1995 was held in a squatted cinema in north London. The large auditorium cinema had been closed down and was awaiting refurbishment by its new corporate owners when it was to be gutted and converted into a six-screen complex. Local authority planning permission had held up the take-over and while it lay empty, a group of free-party people squatted the building. It was not long before an eviction notice was served, but before their departure a large-scale party was set in motion to celebrate their triumph. Squatting places like this in the heart of London were seen as big victories and worthy of celebration.

Entrance to the party was through a small fire exit door at the rear of the building. Here one of the organisers was filtering people through, keeping a close eye on anyone who looked as if they might be from the law enforcement authorities. The front of the building had been boarded up, presumably under the instruction of the owners to keep out unwanted guests. The party spread through the entire building, though the main activity was in the large auditorium part of the cinema, still with the seats running its breadth and depth. The DJ was stationed in the area in front of the screen. The original foyer area had been turned over to a dance floor. Approximately 500 people in various states of consciousness roamed around the vast cinema space. Thrash party attendees were either drunk, on LSD, or completely anaesthetised through the use of ketamine.[7] Corridors and stairwells in the bowels of the building were cold and eerie. Some were congested with gatherings of people and others were completely empty and devoid of life as the huge building struggled to swallow up the numbers. Overall, the place was a health and safety hazard. The toilets were stuffed full of toilet paper and were near to overflowing. If anything had gone wrong in the place it would have been difficult to get people out through the limited exits. With no sense of day and night within the walls of the cinema, the party carried on into the afternoon of the day after.

This form of rave club organisation was certainly being designed and generated by rave club participants. Thus, they could be viewed as active in creating the culture of which they were a part. But because of the free nature of this particular part of the rave culture the only money economy that underpinned it was a drugs economy. Therefore, it has to be viewed in a slightly different light to the other forms of cultural and leisure entrepreneurialism written about in this chapter.

Summary

What I have presented in this chapter is a description of the main event types that were going on in London at the time of my research. This by no means covers all the celebration styles that people were engaged in, but is a fair representation of how the culture had unfolded at this particular point. On top of this, I have provided detailed descriptions of some of the club nights and parties attended over the course of my fieldwork. This has been to give some flavour of the type of environments in which drug use and drug selling were occurring, which the following chapter goes on to describe in more detail. It has also differentiated rave club organisation as that managed by commercial leisure entrepreneurs and that innovated by rave club participants themselves. In the following chapter the drug use patterns occurring among the different groups and people on whom my research was focused are discussed.

Notes

1 O'Hagan (1999, 2004) grouped the proliferation of music styles under three broad types: 'UK garage', 'underground techno and trance' and 'drum 'n' base'.

2 The first significant amendment to legislation was made in July 1990, when the Entertainments (Increased Penalties) Act received royal assent (Collin 1997: 117). This was a specific reaction to the popularity of 'raves', and the realisation that a highly organised drug market had developed alongside them. The Act raised the maximum penalties for holding unlicensed parties to a fine of £20,000 (up from £2,000) and up to six years imprisonment for those responsible for their organisation. According to Collin (1997), although the Act focused on breaches of health and safety, the amendment was an attempt to reduce the large-scale supply and demand for ecstasy. The second noteworthy amendment influencing the organisation of rave club culture was the introduction of the Criminal Justice and Public Order Act. This became law on 3 November 1994 and was directly linked to the ongoing organisation of increasing numbers of illegal 'rave' parties being held around the country. To Collin one of the underlying aims of the Bill was `to usher people back into licensed leisure patterns' (1997: 221).

3 The Public Entertainments Licences (Drug Misuse) Act 1997 was the last in a series of amendments throughout the 1990s aimed at restricting the rave club culture. This piece of legislation achieved royal assent in July 1997 and enabled police to order local authorities to shut down nightclubs where drug using and dealing was known to be occurring. Previously, the process of having a nightclub closed down could take up to two years. This was because of the time it took to get a court hearing and the appeal procedure to which licence holders were entitled. With the introduction of this legislation, the process could be completed within two weeks (Bloomfield 1998).

4 The Anti-Social Behaviour Act, 2003 (www.drugs.gov.uk/Reports and Publications/Communities) further strengthened police powers to close down venues housing drug activity. A particular emphasis was on the closure of 'crack houses', but pubs and clubs were included.

5 Chill-out spaces in clubs provide an area for people to take a rest from the energetic dancing brought on through the use of ecstasy and highly charged club atmospheres.

6 Base speed is amphetamine sulphate powder in its most pure form.

7 Ketamine is an animal tranquilliser which became popular within some sections of the rave club culture (Bellos 1997). Those under its influence were easily identified by their near paralysed state, in contrast to the ecstasy induced energy levels of others around them.

Chapter 3

Friendship network drug-use styles

> I started with speed, acid and alcohol, and downers after it
> . . . It was in a long stretch: it wasn't all at once, obviously.
> (Hammersley *et al.* 2002: 89)

A unique feature of my enquiry into the rave club culture was the long time frame over which it was carried out, and the changes in drug using trends and behaviour observed over time. Different drugs arrived on the scene, and different drugs moved in and out of favour in people's lives. Among the people I came to know, levels of personal use escalated at some points and lessened at others, and the extent to which they were involved in the clubbing lifestyle fluctuated and changed over time.

In the early months of my going out to nightclubs and hanging around with rave club participants most people took ecstasy on a night out and smoked cannabis later on during 'chill-out' sessions. Cocaine was saved for special occasions such as the Christmas holiday period and certain special parties. As time moved on though, cocaine became increasingly popular and was regularly purchased to be used on a night out, as well as on nights in. Ecstasy and later on cocaine were the two drugs that dominated the drug using preferences of the people I observed, but different drug use patterns and preferences were evidenced across the friendship networks. Different groups held different attitudes towards the various drugs on the scene. Joe's friendship group for example, saw nothing wrong with taking substances such as ketamine and LSD on a regular basis, where others considered this type of drug use to be high risk, and also beneath them. Drugs snobbery was a real feature of the rave club scene. People who graduated on to using the supposedly more superior cocaine, looked down on ecstasy users, referring to them as 'e-heads', and most of the people I socialised among looked down on the psychedelic drugs excesses of the free-party scene.

Despite the differences in drug taking, drugs bound the whole culture together and an overriding pattern of sustained use over a period of years was observed; a pattern which some were finding difficult to stop. Most of the people I observed were able to control their drug use and managed to combine it with work, study and other responsibilities, though some let it go unchecked and encountered a series of problems as a consequence.

In this chapter I describe the general drug use styles of the key characters and their friendship groups to give a sense of the drug use cultures that were going on as a part of the London rave club scene.

Joe's free-party group and poly-drug use

The following describes Joe's group's drugs use style. It was through my hanging around with Andy that I became familiar with the different people in Joe's group. I went to a few Thrash parties they attended, but in the main my socialising alongside this group was playing games of pool in pubs prior to them heading out on their weekend party excursions. Joe's group didn't overlap in any significant way with the other friendship groups I socialised among, quite likely due to their very different clubbing and drug use styles.

Joe's friendship group was large in number. Joe was a central figure within this friendship group. This was based on his position as drug seller to them. Virtually all the group, the women included, were heavy drug users. The drug using style of club-goers came to be described as poly-drug use, but this group were the most 'poly' of drug users on whom my observations were based. They took anything as long as it was cheap. Their favourites were base speed, LSD, ecstasy tablets, magic mushrooms, when in season, and some of the more hardened members enjoyed ketamine. Base speed was popular, mainly because of its cheapness in relation to the duration of the high. A gram of base speed purchased off Joe was £10 and was enough to keep you going all night and much of the next day too. As the months passed, a few people in the group moved onto taking cocaine. They'd initially frowned on cocaine use. Few could afford it, but really they didn't view it as a party drug. As cocaine became more available, and crucially more affordable, it began to permeate this group's drug using repertoires as rapidly as it moved into the other groups.

This friendship network socialised in numbers of about twenty, regularly attending Thrash parties and other squat parties in and around London. Occasionally they went to nightclubs but only ones where the entry fee was cheap. In their terms this ruled out most of them. Due to the hidden nature of the parties they attended, drug selling and drug use at them went unsupervised. Only other partygoers monitored each other's well-being and states of consciousness. Given that most were as reckless as each other there was little group disdain at the heavy levels of use. Drug use was by and large hedonist, uncaring and sustained over long periods. Party sessions began on Friday nights, and didn't finish until late on Sunday night, with lull periods spent in pubs drinking large amounts of alcohol. It was not unusual for the whole list of substances to be consumed over the course of a party session. Depending on individual tolerance, it was nothing for both men and women to consume upwards of two grams of base speed, four to five ecstasy tablets and a tab of LSD over a weekend party session.

Joe's group's drug use was by far the most reckless of the different friendship networks, but Robin's was another one notable for its cavalier use. Robin's friendship network was largely made up of young Australasians living and working in London on the two-year working holiday visa. I regularly socialised alongside them at the Pace Bar. It was through frequent gatherings at the Pace Bar, the Venus Group dance parties, and around at each other's houses that I observed the precise organisation of this group's drugs using and purchasing practices.

A group of young Australasians and heavy ecstasy use

In the same way as Joe was the central person within his group based on his role as drug seller to them, Robin was a key figure in her group. Robin had been a part of the Australian rave club culture and had been selling drugs, on and off back there. It was not long after arriving in London in 1996 that she found herself back where she had left off, and was selling ecstasy pills, speed, cocaine and cannabis to various people she knew who wanted them. The strong bonds of the Australasian travelling culture in London combined with the camaraderie of the rave club culture meant this group grew in size by the day. New arrivals to London, plus many others, were drawn into the fold. Robin's friends found the London nightclub culture something quite unlike anything they had experienced back home, plus they found the drugs to be much cheaper here than they were in Australia. One of the girls commented: 'It's $150 [£70–75 using the exchange rate of the time] Australian for a gram [of cocaine] back home and not that good'.

Seeing they were in London for a finite period, Robin's group launched headlong into its rave scene. They went out most weekends and sometimes during the week too. They thought nothing of taking five ecstasy tablets on a night out. Drug dosage varied from person to person, but one or two, possibly three tablets, over the course of a night, was the most common. At the time of my fieldwork, purity tests on ecstasy tablets usually found them to contain levels of MDMA between 75mg to 125mg. It was this amount that was said to achieve the optimum effects of the drug, such as euphoria, empathy and feelings of closeness (Saunders 1993). In the years since, anecdotal reports state the quality of ecstasy tablets are low. Two to three tablets would have been a high dose in the years of the late 1990s, this is not now considered to be the case.[1]

Being newcomers to the scene, this group had nothing to go by to gauge what was a normal dose and for a while some took five tablets on a night out and what was more, boasted about it. Ned was one young Australian who on a night out regularly consumed ecstasy tablets like sweets and was often heard the next day comparing doses with his friends: 'How many pills did you do last night?', 'Aar, I did five, my legs were like jelly, but it was wicked man'. They didn't keep this up for long. As time moved on, those in the group who continued to take this many tablets in a session were beginning to be viewed by the others as a liability to steer clear of. Even though this was a drugs culture that did little to hide itself, it was still important not to draw unwanted attention to yourself and those people whose behaviour was deemed to be doing so, were told to 'sort it out', or were simply pushed out of the group. It seemed the temporary and holiday-like nature of their stay in London encouraged members of Robin's group to take as many drugs as they could and as often as they could, knowing the party would be over the day they got on the plane to return home. Robin describes the party style her group got into:

> All of our mates, when they first arrived here, all went a bit crazy, and now they are just 'chilling out' a bit. Don't want to fuck themselves up as much, and don't have the need. That was last year sort of thing and this is this year. We are sort of on a different vibe, we sort of did the full dance party circuit when we got here and went and checked out all the clubs and I suppose the Es just went hand and hand with it all.

This group's clubbing and drug-taking lifestyle had a natural end to it, or it was at least likely to change on their return home, but there were a few people among the different friendship groups who were finding the club drug-taking lifestyle difficult to put an end to.

It is not uncommon for recreational styles of drug use to be entered into in the late teen years, which then tail off in the early twenties as increasing domestic and work responsibilities become a part of life. But a dominant pattern of drug use within this leisure culture was that of sustained use, over a long period of time, as well as into an older age. Some people positioned themselves on the periphery of the scene, dipping in and out of drug use in line with their nights out clubbing. Others became entrenched clubbers and drug takers over a long period of time. Andy and some members of his early friendship group can be described in this way.

Andy: a sustained drug user

In 1998, by the time my fieldwork among the different overlapping friendship networks was over, Andy and some of his friends had notched up a long history of clubbing and drug taking. They started going out clubbing at age 17, and eight years later at age 25 a few of them continued to go out most weekends and sometimes through the week too. In the early years, Andy and his friends mostly took one to two ecstasy tablets on a night out and sometimes small amounts of cocaine. Occasionally he and a friend clubbed together to buy a gram, but on their low earnings they were rarely able to afford it.

It was when Andy moved to live in London in 1994 at age 21 that his busy mover lifestyle and accompanying drugs socialising, took off. Prior to this, Andy lived in the outer suburbs of south London and getting to rave clubs took time and effort. He and his friends made regular nightclub outings, and took the range of drugs they did in all manner of places, such as in friend's bedrooms, parks, pubs, and at house parties, but their drugs lifestyles were tempered by living at home with parents. On moving to live independently in London, Andy's busy mover drugs lifestyle could be conducted with relative freedom and rave clubs and party venues were on his doorstep. Plus, the pool of clubbers and new friends he could link in with was endless. This ease of drugs activity connects to a point I make throughout this book. This is that the large population size of London and its accompanying anonymity, made many of the drugs trading relations and interactions possible.

It was from this point that Andy's selling moved up a notch from low-level friendship group drug sales to obliging almost anybody he met who wanted them. The downside for Andy, even with this low-level selling, was it kept him tied to other drug takers and made it difficult to resist taking drugs himself. At age 25, he continued to take ecstasy most weekends and even though he was unable to afford cocaine, the large number of friends he had who either sold it, or regularly had it in their possession, helped out with that.

Andy's story was a common one. Many people in these friendship networks were drawn into the rave club lifestyle in their late teens and early 20s, and by the time my research was complete, Andy had been using ecstasy and cocaine for close on ten years. Occasionally periods of moderation were imposed, usually following spells of excessive use, but overall a consistent pattern of drug taking had developed, and this was regardless of age. Andy's group were young people aging into drugs use through their 20s, but there were older clubbers who had long drug using histories which were following them well into their 30s and beyond.

This can be said of Tom's friendship network. Tom's group had come upon the rave club culture at an older age, in their mid 20s and in their early 30s they continued to take drugs at an insatiable rate. The difference here was that cocaine was their drug of choice. They took it not only when they were out clubbing, but wherever and whenever it took their fancy.

Tom's group: an older group of clubber's drug use

There were other people around whom groups gathered. This was not connected to their drug supplies, but to their entrepreneurship and organisation of rave club type events. This was how it was for Tom. He was a central person in his friendship group, based on being the main organiser of the Venus Group dance parties. Tom's friendship network was not one of the five on whom my observations were centred, but they often drank at the Pace Bar and they were dedicated supporters of Venus Group events. With that I came to know different people within the group. The number of people who aligned themselves to Tom was many, but he had a fixed friendship group. These were his long-time friends. They were an older aged group. Rave club friendship groups could evolve over a short period of time, and on not much more than being a part of the same club drugs culture, but Tom's group was one of genuine friends and was closed to outsiders. They were not interested in welcoming newcomers, and with their older age they had a different attitude towards participating in the rave club scene. Theirs was an elite participation.

Tom's core group was a network of men and women aged in their early 30s. They were mainly white and numbered about ten in total. The majority were in established jobs and well paid ones at that. One was a lawyer, one was a medical doctor, one was a chartered surveyor and another was an architect. This group was moneyed compared to the other friendship groups. They owned cars and flats, went on holidays, were in long-term relationships and a couple of them had started families. Most were Londoners. They were keen cocaine users and drank heavily. Sometimes they took ecstasy, but generally cocaine was the drug of choice.

This tight-knit friendship group had established an ongoing pattern of socialising out in bars and clubs both on the weekends and during the week too. They managed their partying alongside the full-time jobs most of them held. They were easily able to afford cocaine and had taken it from early on in their clubbing careers. In addition to their regular cocaine-using gatherings, this group enjoyed elongated party excursions. Their celebrating regularly continued after a club event around at one of their homes and often into Sunday evening.

One night in early 1997 when I was out at a club event alongside this group I was invited back to an after party at one of their homes. After parties often ended up with a few people who were only loosely connected, but Tom's group was a closed circle and outsiders were rarely invited to join.

Once we arrived at the house, money was pooled for supplies of vodka and whisky to be purchased from the local off-licence, and more ecstasy tablets and cocaine were being consumed. After party people usually knew of an off-licence that sold alcohol outside of the regulation hours and there was one nearby well known for its middle of the night opening hours and which sold whatever alcohol you wanted. These were the days of the Seabreeze cocktail which was a generous shot of Vodka mixed with cranberry juice and grapefruit juice. Many of these were being drunk. Drug consumption at after parties differed by person. Some used these gatherings to relax and wind down after the club event. Others used them as an opportunity to extend the party vibe. Most of this bunch were using this one to carry on the party. There was a slight unease among some of the group at my presence. This was connected to my outsider status and what I associated with the way cocaine sharing rituals become established among friendship groups. This group regularly socialised together and with that openly shared their supplies with each other. But, on this occasion, the presence of someone they didn't know that well meant having to execute cocaine sniffing sessions out of sight in a different room. I left them around eight o'clock in the morning, but in their usual style this lot continued late into Sunday afternoon and evening. They often finished off their weekend's drug use with a dose of temazepan late on Sunday night, to help them sleep the night through. Sleep was not something easily managed after a weekend of cocaine snorting.

Extended clubbing sessions and drug taking

Long clubbing excursions were not only a feature of Tom's group. As the rave club culture opened out, extended clubbing excursions became the norm. Previously a club outing was meeting in a pub prior to going to the club, and afterwards going back to someone's house for a chill-out session. These usually involved drinking tea and smoking cannabis until the first early morning underground trains started running or until people felt straight enough to drive home again.

Not far down the line, the after party emerged, which extended club outings well into the following day and sometimes longer than that. Here, various drugs were consumed and often large quantities of alcohol were drunk.

Initially after party sessions were mostly held at people's houses but they increasingly came to be held out in commercial, public venues. Groups of dishevelled clubbers were often in the Pace Bar on

Saturday and Sunday mornings, not having made it home from the previous night's clubbing and still wearing their club clothes. The ambient DJ tunes were soaked up as the effects of ecstasy use gave way to the numbing effects of alcohol. More and more commercial venues equipped themselves to profit from this extended style of rave club socialising. Bars installed DJs to play and some clubs even opened their doors at 8.00 am, or earlier, on Saturday and Sunday mornings, and staying open into the later evening to cater for this demand.

Robin's group frequently spent their after party sessions out in bars and clubs around north London and with this got into a pattern of extended drinking and drug use sessions. These continued long into the following day after a night out. Most of the people in Robin's friendship group were new to the London rave club culture and in their awe at it embraced it with enthusiasm. A common scenario on entry into the club scene was to engage in a period of enthusiastic partying before a more cautious approach was applied further down the line (Collin 1997). This group was still in the early stages of involvement, and every club and party session that came up was cause for celebration.

Through the lively atmosphere of the Pace Bar it was during 1997 and 1998 that Robin's friendship group of young Australasians merged with Rex's group, and Andy also became a central figure. Robin and Rex's group's after parties involved heavy drinking, heavy cannabis smoking and over the months the more hardy of them began taking ecstasy as well. Sometimes they prepared for the after party in advance. Stocks of alcohol, usually vodka, and cannabis were purchased, ready for the return home in the morning. It didn't matter if they hadn't prepared. By the time they got back from their club excursion, it was usually past seven o'clock in the morning and the local off-licence was open and willing to sell alcohol to them. In respect to cannabis, there was always someone in the group who had some on them. If not, it was easy enough to make a phone call to order some in. Dealers were quick to capitalise on this new opening in the drugs market, and some made their mobile numbers available to be phoned in the early hours to provide a service.

This group operated in a way where the first few hours of the after party was spent lounging about smoking large amounts of cannabis and drinking vodka cocktails. Different male members of the group took turns mixing techno tunes on the turntables. Around midday they slowly moved on to a local bar or pub, where they spent the rest of the afternoon and usually the evening too. Some of the group dropped off along the way, but it was more common for this group to grow in size over the day as other friends joined in too. As much as Tom's group's after parties were closed affairs, Robin's and Rex's were open-ended, made up of the friends they had gone out with, plus any others who cared to join in. The Pace Bar became a regular Sunday after party meeting place. It often turned into a full-scale celebration by Sunday evening as the last hours of the weekend were taken advantage of before the return to work on Monday morning.

Clubbing and increasing cocaine use

Earlier, I mentioned the increasing cocaine use that was occurring within the rave club culture. Initially cocaine had been restricted to more moneyed crowds, such as Tom's group, or saved for special occasions. As the months and years of my observations passed by, it began to feature in many people's drug-using lives. All of a sudden around 1997 it was everywhere and more and more people were using it. In the same way as large numbers of people became involved in the supply of ecstasy tablets, which had the effect of pushing the price down from £15 to £12 to £10 over a short time period,[2] the same happened with cocaine. Previously cocaine had been selling at £60 a gram, but it dropped to between £45 and £50, and even lower if you knew somebody who sold it. Such decreases were making it more accessible to greater numbers of people. Though rather than it replacing ecstasy, many people used it as well. By and large, people restricted ecstasy use to weekends, but cocaine was used midweek and accompanied any range of social activities, from watching TV at a friend's house, to having a drink down the pub. A common feeling among people who moved on to taking cocaine was that functioning was less impaired the following day when compared to ecstasy. A line heard in its favour was 'you can get up in the morning', and the perception of this greater level of operation formed the argument behind many people's transition.

As cocaine became more available, and with many more people taking it, people shifted from treating it as a special occasion drug and using it sparingly, to taking it on a regular basis. People were pooling their funds and buying a gram whenever the mood took them. However, even though cocaine decreased in price, it was still expensive in comparison to other drugs and realistically many were unable to afford it. This especially applied to younger rave club participants such as Andy's early friendship group, most of whom were living on meagre incomes or borrowing heavily against student loans to fund the cost of their clubbing lifestyles. People might have found taking cocaine enabled them to carry on as normal the following day, but problems were emerging in what it was doing to their finances.

The greater popularity of cocaine was also reflected in nightclub drug sales. Where previously it had only been possible to purchase ecstasy tablets in nightclubs, cocaine was increasingly added to the list of drugs nightclub sellers had available. There was a hazard with this though. The sweltering and humid conditions in most clubs made having cocaine on your person an expensive risk to take. Under damp conditions cocaine easily crystallised, rendering it useless for sniffing and certainly for sale. At a Venus Group party in 1997 Andy lost the £60 gram wrap of cocaine he'd taken along. In the hot and moist atmosphere, it had turned to a small solid block in his back pocket.

Further evidence of the growing popularity of cocaine was the rising demand for it within friendship groups. Those who were involved in low-level purchasing and selling were increasingly being asked to access cocaine on their friends' behalf. The majority of people in the different friendship groups I observed reserved cocaine for special occasions or managed to keep their use under control, but a few let it go unchecked and found themselves having to rein it in (Shaffer and Jones 1989; Waldorf et al. 1991; Ditton and Hammersley 1996). Colin was one of these.

Colin's heavy cocaine use

A couple of years after meeting Colin in 1993, his social life began to take a different turn. He began working as a barman in a commercial London nightclub and alongside the job was using increasing quantities of ecstasy tablets and cocaine. Moreover, his cocaine use had come to be a problem. Colin's drift into problem cocaine use was one of quick progression, from taking two to three ecstasy tablets on a Friday night while out at Lush, to two years later sniffing over a gram a day and selling it to cover the cost. Colin had been taking drugs prior to his participation in the London rave club culture and often mentioned the earlier time in Australia when he 'took lots of speed'. Things shifted up a level for Colin when he moved into his nightclub job. Working in the club meant he was not only surrounded by people taking ecstasy and cocaine, but he was also close to the club dealers who supplied them. Colin began taking cocaine purchased cheaply through the club dealers and his door security colleagues on the nights he worked, as well as on the nights he didn't. 'The coke dealer sells to me for £20 a gram and the bouncers sell me what they confiscate off the punters, for cheap'. He continued with this pattern of heavy cocaine use for more than two years and while he was able to hold down his job, he was coming up against a string of other problems as a result. The pivotal point was in early 1998 when he was caught in possession of four one gram wraps of cocaine. Previous attempts to rein his cocaine taking in had failed, but being arrested was the point when he managed it.

Colin's case highlights the relative ease in the way people progressed on to heavier forms of drug use. It also illustrates the way in which entering into drug selling within this leisure culture was a relatively straightforward transition to make. Robin had found this. She commented that selling drugs on a larger scale had 'kind of just happened'. She explained this through the number of people in her friendship network who were keen to purchase them, but who were unable to access a supply themselves.

> All my mates were doing it, and a lot of my close friends needed drug supplies and I sort of ended up picking up for them, so picking up five or six pills and a few grams of speed. It was cheaper to buy in quarters and buy in bulk, so it just seemed logical for me to go and get as much as I could with the amount of money that I had, and I sort of just fell into it.

Aaron's problem drug use

Aaron was someone else who experienced an escalation in his drug use. His went further though and he was forced to seek help with it. Aaron was a main supplier at various moving dance parties and for a while operated as a main seller of ecstasy and cocaine at the Venus Group parties. Aaron was a peripheral member of Robin, Rex and Mick's overlapping friendship network and frequently drank at the Pace Bar.

He was a London man, in his early 40s. He didn't work, not in the legitimate sense anyway. Selling drugs was his work. For some time he'd made money as a drugs seller and this coincided with heavy drug use.

Aaron was often 'stoned', whether he was selling at a dance party, or whether it was the middle of the day going about his everyday business. Aaron's drug use crossed the line of being under control when he made the transition from taking ecstasy and cocaine, to smoking 'crack' cocaine on a daily basis. This was a style of drug use that had moved beyond what his extended social network considered acceptable. Those who had previously socialised with him and who at the time were grateful for his ready supply of cocaine and other drugs were moving away from him. Examples like this can be linked to the notion of functionality as it existed within some social relationships, in this drugs culture. Drug exchange was largely bound up within conceptions of friendship, but the instrumental nature of the buying and selling relationship was sometimes revealed. The lines between the role of a drug seller and friends as customers, having previously been blurred, on occasions became separated – so that their friends remained keen to access drugs and not much more.

It was evident that heavy drug use was part and parcel of a drug-selling lifestyle. Excessive drug use among sellers occurred for the simple reason that they were surrounded by them, they could use them at little financial cost, and most of their relationships, friendships and reason for existence at that point in time centred on their status as a seller. This was the situation Mick found himself in, and indeed in difficulty controlling his use.

Mick as a user dealer

Mick's friendship group was one of the three groups that regularly socialised at the Pace Bar through 1997 and 1998, and along with that comprised members of Robin's and Rex's group. Mick was a key person within the group connected to the role he played in drug selling and the way groups naturally formed around a person who had a drug supply. Mick had sold cannabis to a steady flow of customers for a few years, but this expanded to include cocaine and sometimes ecstasy too.

In line with this enlarged operation, Mick's drug use increased. Previously he'd been a daily cannabis smoker and on the weekends shared a gram or two of cocaine with his friends, but along with his move into selling cocaine Mick was using it more and more frequently. He took it most nights of the week, and Friday and Saturday nights often turned into whole-night drug using sessions. This was because it was constantly in his possession and more of his time was spent co-ordinating purchases connected to it. It was not helped by the penchant his friends had also developed for it. This was a pattern observed across other groups too. When someone within a group moved into a more full-time style of drug selling, the rest of the group's drug taking moved in an upward direction. Selling significant amounts of cocaine or ecstasy meant buying them at cheaper rates. The more you bought, the cheaper the price paid. Mick passed this reduction on to his friends, and being able to purchase it at a more affordable price, meant that they too moved on to take it more frequently. It took strength of character for those who were friends with dealers to resist the cheap drug offers and ready supplies.

Mick had previously not concerned himself with thoughts of quitting the selling lifestyle, but with the larger amounts of cocaine he was using and the difficulty he was having controlling it, he regularly mentioned 'giving it up'. He recognised the Catch 22 situation he was in (Waldorf 1993), but changing things was easier said than done.

Rave club lifestyles and health problems

Initially people were reluctant to make an association between the areas that were going wrong in their lives and the drug and party lifestyles they were living. This was simply because they were having too much fun, and admitting it would in theory mean having to change it. Some though found they could no longer deny the connection. This was the case with Colin and Mick who were forced to address the impact their cocaine use was having on their lives. The heavy drinking culture that was emerging as a part of rave club lifestyles was also causing problems for a few. The early convention that alcohol was largely avoided by rave club participants while out taking ecstasy (Merchant and MacDonald 1994; Collin 1997; McElrath and McEvoy 1999; Measham *et al.* 2001) was not the case a few years later. High levels of alcohol were consumed before and during club events, as well as afterwards to aid the 'come down' from the ecstasy and/or cocaine high (Sherlock and Conner 1999; Winstock *et al.* 2001; Deehan and Saville 2003; Riley and Hayward 2004).

Patterns of heavy midweek drinking were also established. People congregated in their favourite DJ bars to reminisce about the previous weekend's clubbing, to plan the next one, and in support of their friends who DJed in them. Drinking cultures are established in complex ways, but the expansion in the social spaces and venues in which this culture was being celebrated helped to encourage patterns of socialising that also involved heavy drinking.

Heavy drinking as a part of the rave club culture was also being fuelled by the growing numbers of people using cocaine. Alcohol and cocaine went hand-in-hand. Boys and colleagues (2002) noted this in their small-scale study of cocaine use among young Londoners. They found alcohol was often consumed at double the usual rate if cocaine had been used. In explaining this, they noted the compound 'cocaethylene' produced in the body when cocaine and alcohol (ethanol) were used together. They reported cocaethylene produced 'greater euphoria and psychological well being' than when either substance was used separately (McCance-Katz *et al.* 1998: cited in Boys *et al.* 2002: 203). It seemed that those I was observing who were partaking in this cocktail would agree with this finding (*cf.* Pearson 2001; Korf *et al.* 2003).

Stan was one person I came to know who enjoyed this mix, but who ran into problems with it.

Stan as a heavy drinker and drug user

Stan was located within the large friendship network comprising Robin, Rex and Mick's contacts. He regularly socialised at the Pace Bar, Venus Group parties, and at various other rave club events. He was 21, white and hadn't long lived in London when I met him in mid 1997. He'd recently moved down from his hometown in Scotland and had initially come on a student internship. But not long after being in London he resigned from his studies opting for a lifestyle of going out clubbing and selling drugs. Stan had been part of the Scottish rave club culture which was known for its hard-edge style (Reynolds 1998: 87) and Stan's stamina for partying verified it.[3]

Along with the expansion in social spaces in which the rave club scene was being celebrated, bars and pubs became popular places for the exchange and purchase of ecstasy tablets and cocaine. The general format that existed around selling in these arenas involved the person locating themselves out in them, waiting for customers to turn up, either by prior arrangement or drawing people in simply by being there with drugs on their person. Stan operated in this way. He regularly spent whole weekends out and about sniffing cocaine, drinking large amounts of vodka, smoking copious cigarettes, as he moved between different bars, pubs and dance parties, selling his ecstasy and cocaine supplies. Stan kept this up for a couple of years, but at a certain point his body could no longer tolerate the excesses and he suffered from pancreatitis; a medical condition linked to excess alcohol consumption. This serious knock to his health made it difficult to deny the damage the cocaine and alcohol lifestyle was causing him. But these were difficult admissions to make. People's whole lives were bound up with this leisure culture and making a transition to a less involved lifestyle was difficult, especially for those who had occupational roles within it, such as being a drug seller.

Mental ill-health and drug use

Davie was another person who couldn't deny the negative impact his drug use was having. He was someone who experienced mental ill-health in connection to his recreational club drug use. Davie was a peripheral member of the large social network, though he was more linked to outer members of Mick's group. Davie was a London raised, white 23 year old. He worked in the film industry, and like his friends, he enjoyed taking drugs. But he was one of a handful of people met over the course of my research who experienced mental illness directly attributable to their drug use.

Concerns were raised during the 1990s on the increasing number of admissions to psychiatric services by young people. Specialists linked this to the rising use of stimulant and hallucinogenic drugs such as ecstasy, speed, and LSD, which it was believed, could trigger latent mental illness (Lehane and Rees 1996; Thompson 1996). Precisely because of their youth, young people were not to know whether they were susceptible to mental ill-health. While some could take drugs without serious effect, others were vulnerable. This was the case with Davie. Along with his friends Davie had been taking ecstasy, cocaine, occasionally LSD, and smoking cannabis since his late teens. One afternoon in 1998 when he and his friends were at an outdoor music event, they took LSD. Davie spiralled into a state of disorientation which lasted a number of days, and eventually led to his admission to a private psychiatric hospital.

There were other areas of people's lives that were being affected. A few people failed to hold on to their jobs, or stay on top of their studies, and some were arrested in possession of different dance drugs with varying penalties attached. Andy was continuously in and out of jobs. Lateness and general unreliability led to him being moved on from a handful of jobs, and he simply walked out of a college course he later got on to, a few months after beginning it. Although rarely admitting it, those who were students and combining their studying with partying, struggled to run the two together. This was illustrated in the case of Stan. He pulled out of university to resolve the clash between the two. Nathan, Robin's boyfriend, also dropped out of the degree course he was on. The quality of his work and general attendance was deteriorating. Joe was another example. He was more calculated in his withdrawal from university, but pulling out of his degree studies for a year, was in part down to not being able to keep up with the demands of his course while engaging in the clubbing lifestyle.

Most people I observed were able to control their drug use and managed to combine it alongside their other life responsibilities, though some let it go unchecked and encountered a range of problems as a consequence; problems which indeed caused a reining in, or quitting of drug use.

Summary

By and large the rave club drugs culture is referred to as a recreational drugs culture which people manage alongside their work and other lives, and whose drug use causes them little harm. My observations revealed that plenty of people were coming to no harm with the drugs they were using and the frequency with which they used them, yet there were many who were encountering different problems, directly attributable to their rave drug lifestyles. This included health, domestic, financial and legal problems. In this way, it is my argument that the lines between recreational and problematic drug use within this culture were sometimes difficult to draw, and blurred for some people at some points.

Notes

1 A study carried out among a sample of London-based recreational drug users found a range 0.5–14 ecstasy tablets taken on a session out, with an overall average of three tablets being used (Moskalewicz *et al.* 2009).
2 In the early months of my research in 1993, ecstasy pills were a standard £15 per tablet. Within a year they dropped to £12 and a year later again they were down to £10.
3 Stan's illness occurred after I had formally withdrawn from 'the field', but my contact with a number of people on whom my observations had been based, were ongoing. It was through a continued interest in their lifestyles

that this incident was recorded. This can be related to the process of 'leaving the field' as it occurs in anthropological research. Fieldwork can be ongoing in an informal way years after leaving the field, as noted by Watson (1999).

Chapter 4

Drug selling in London rave clubs

> . . . everyone was doing it – everyone was a drug dealer.
> Whether it was three or thirty, they were still selling.
> (Collin 1997: 70)

The following two chapters describe and discuss the way drugs were bought and sold in the rave club scene. A knock-on effect of the widespread drug use going on as a part of the rave club culture was the large numbers of people who became involved in selling them. Small and large-scale operations were entered into with ease, and the opportunities to profit from club floor and social network drug sales were seized upon.

My observations of drug selling and purchasing are essentially differentiated by selling in the more 'risky' public domain such as in nightclubs and dance parties, and drug selling in the safer confines of the private domain – that which is among known contacts within social and friendship networks and which takes place in more discreet and hidden locations. These include people's homes, pubs and bars, workplaces and as other disguised activities; such as meeting out on the street or in the aisle of a busy local supermarket.

This chapter deals with drugs trading in clubs and at dance parties and the following chapter discusses social network drug selling. It is difficult to locate sellers precisely in one or other of these spheres. People who located their sales in clubs and dance parties didn't isolate their selling to this arena, and those who took part in social network selling sometimes took up opportunities to sell in clubs and at dance parties.

Interwoven with these descriptions are the way risk and safety was observed in regard to the exchange of drugs in these different contexts. A key safety issue for drugs dealers is maintaining a low profile in order not to be caught. This is achieved in a range of obvious and less obvious ways. There are also expectations on purchasers to assist in concealing a drugs dealer's identity. It is vital that drugs dealers' activities are kept discreet and there are unwritten rules surrounding the way people behave and interact with them.

Drug selling in nightclubs

Corresponding with the high level of demand for ecstasy and other stimulant drugs from within the rave club culture, drug selling in nightclubs was commonplace, and because of the centrality of drugs to a night out, the success of a club night could depend on whether there was a supply on the premises. This was widely recognised among nightclub promoters and dance party organisers, and regardless of venue type some way of securing such a supply had usually been arranged. In some clubs it was evident but discreet, and in other clubs it wasn't uncommon to hear dealers reeling off the list of drugs they had available as you walked past them – 'Es, charlie, speed'.

Drug supply in clubs took a range of forms. In some it was a highly organised operation and was tied into the nightclub management structure. In others it was more of a free-for-all and any number of commercial sellers could turn up to sell their wares. From my observations three different nightclub seller types were identified.

First, there were those whom I call *resident dealers*. These operated with the consent of the club management and either worked as employees or, more typically, worked in some form of partnership arrangement with them. Partnership arrangements were sometimes organised by the security staff hired to control the door. In either arrangement part of the security staff function was to search customers on entry into the club. This was to deter unauthorised dealers from coming in and entering into competition with the resident dealers. Resident dealers usually paid a fee to secure sole selling rights in the club.

The second type of club-based dealer identified were those I refer to as *club dealers*. These worked either as independent sellers or in

73

small networks and sold in different clubs and dance parties. Club dealers researched the London nightclub terrain, locating the best clubs to sell in, learning the different club security systems in place and simply turned up like any other 'clubber', but with a bag of ecstasy tablets to sell. These were transient, freelance salespeople. Some clubs turned a blind eye to them. Other clubs worked hard to filter them out. Having sold their merchandise, club dealers either moved on to another club where they did the same thing there, or ended their night's selling at that point to enjoy their own night clubbing.

The third type of club-based dealer was the *opportunistic seller* who was someone attending the club as a customer, but who smuggled small quantities of drugs past the door security to sell inside the club. This usually covered the cost of the evening's entertainment. Opportunistic selling was sometimes an extension of friendship networks of dealing, where surplus drugs purchased in anticipation of friends' needs which remained unsold were then sold on in clubs to make back the outlay.

For issues of trust and safety, most people found it preferable to purchase their drug supplies from a known dealer prior to going out to a nightclub, though for different reasons it wasn't always possible. The decision to go to a club was often a spontaneous one, leaving little time to accomplish the time-consuming task of locating ecstasy tablets for the night out. And, it required someone within the friendship group having access to a supply, and many people were not in the position to directly contact a seller in the private domain. Participation in the rave club culture generally meant knowing someone from whom drugs could be purchased, but for security reasons, dealers restricted those who had direct access to them. Those unable to make contact with dealers beforehand were forced to purchase their drugs from anonymous dealers in nightclubs – from one of the three dealer types noted.

Resident dealers

Ronnie and Vince were resident dealers. They were the two main Lush dealers. Lush has been described as an example of a small venue club night. It was through my weekly attendance at Lush over a ten-month period from late in 1993 that I became familiar with Ronnie and Vince and the intricate drug-selling system they operated within the club. My knowledge was also aided by Colin whose regular presence at Lush, and whose keen appetite for ecstasy led to him befriending Ronnie and Vince, and to him playing an informal role in their selling set-up within the club. This was remunerated with free or cheap ecstasy tablets.

Lush was managed and run by a father and his two sons. Ronnie and Vince were friends of the two sons. They were aged 20, were white and were from the local south east London area where the club was located. Both were techno-music fans and regularly took ecstasy. Neither Ronnie nor Vince had jobs. Drug selling was their job. Earlier, Vince had been enrolled on a government training scheme learning carpentry, but the money he made selling drugs far outweighed the time and effort involved in pursuing jobs training. Ronnie had also given up on skills training in favour of selling drugs.

These two had been given the selling rights in Lush and along with a few helpers were there each Friday night selling their high quality supplies of ecstasy tablets. Lush operated differently to other nightclubs with resident dealer systems. Ronnie and Vince were part of the staffing structure. Ronnie ran the cloakroom. This was useful. It meant there were all manner of hiding places to conceal the bags of ecstasy pills and the money being collected over the course of the night.

The cloakroom at Lush doubled up as a drug selling point. Ronnie took care of the cloakroom sales, which he managed alongside checking in the coats and bags, and Vince looked after the floor sales. It was possible to turn up at Lush, queue up to put your coat in and buy your ecstasy supplies for the night at the same time. Vince was more of a roaming seller, though he usually based himself down the back of the club by the toilets. Nightclub sellers often took up a fixed position where they stood for the duration of the evening. This was so if someone who had purchased from them, was asked by anyone else about pill availability, they could easily direct them to the likes of Vince down the back. Exchange of information between clubbers on the accessibility and quality of drugs within clubs was common – 'Do you know anyone who's selling pills?' In the case of Lush it was known to direct enquirers to the back of the club where they found either Ronnie in the cloakroom, or Vince.

A reasonable estimate was that Ronnie and Vince sold between 400 and 600 ecstasy tablets a night. Lush drew a repeat crowd in that the same people turned up each week. In this way most people had come to know these two as the resident dealers. Their numerous sales were also assisted by the particular surveillance they had in place. Most clubs with a resident dealer system used door security staff to check that unofficial sellers didn't infiltrate and to ensure drug sales remained in the hands of the assigned dealers. Lush had a different system. They employed minimal security and didn't impose searches on the door. Ronnie and Vince had their own surveillance operation. No one else was permitted to sell on their territory and a range of tactics were set up to make sure of it. One strategy was that if someone was suspected of selling on the premises, one of their helpers masqueraded as a legitimate customer and asked the person under suspicion 'have you got any pills for sale?' If the response was yes, they were ordered to stop, and with these guys you certainly took notice. Tactics like these meant those looking to purchase, were steered towards Ronnie and Vince alone. This was actually how Colin met Andy in Lush. Colin's role in helping Ronnie and Vince was assisting direct buyers to Ronnie and Vince, and he also helped warn unwitting customers not to sell on their territory. On this night, Colin was alerted to Andy's movements in preparing an exchange and warned him off it – 'make sure you don't sell on these guys patch mate, they won't have it, bring your own along, but don't sell!'

Ronnie and Vince made big profits through their Lush operation. At this level of the drugs market, ecstasy tablets were sold in units of 100 at a time, increasing to units of 1,000, higher up the scale. The cost per tablet decreased with the larger amount purchased (Pearson and Hobbs 2001). Ronnie and Vince purchased in 1,000 tablet amounts and were paying £6 a tablet. Tablets at Lush sold for £15, which was the going rate at this stage in the life of the rave club scene. As I noted, over the course of my field observations there was a large degree of fluctuation in drug prices. In the beginning, in 1993, the standard retail price for an ecstasy tablet was £15. Within a short period this dropped to £12 and then £10. Owing to these price fluctuations, and the different time periods at which I was observing drug purchasing and selling, different prices are quoted throughout this book.

Selling between 400 and 600 tablets a night at £15 each, meant Ronnie and Vince made profits in the region of £3,600 to £4,500 a night. In further maximising their profits, they also began selling £20 'wraps' of cocaine and £10 bags of cannabis. In line with the difficulty of cocaine ingestion in sweltering, damp clubs, and the pungent smell of cannabis smoking, these sales were mainly intended for takeaway use in chill-out sessions after the club. Ronnie and Vince split the profits and fixed payments of £50 were made to the helpers assisting on the night. How much they paid for the privilege of selling in the club wasn't known, but with the profits they made it was likely to be a sizeable amount.

Drug selling in clubs like Lush was obviously high risk, but one advantage with this club in terms of avoiding detection and enforcement activity was its hidden away location. Located behind a black entrance door under a railway arch, those not aware of it being a club would have no idea of the festivities and drugs excesses that lay within. One thing the Lush security did pay attention to was making sure attendees didn't attract unwanted interest to the venue. This was evidenced one night when Andy's friend – Max – collapsed at Lush. He'd been drinking pints of beer, and the high strength ecstasy tablets he'd taken didn't combine well with the alcohol. In these steaming, packed clubs the usual thing to do in this situation was to get the person to a cooler part of the club, but Lush had no such place. The whole club sweltered in dangerously hot temperatures and crammed conditions. A couple of friends got Max to the other side of the entrance door, onto the pavement but were firmly told by the Lush security to 'move him down the road, away from the club'. This was so if any passers-by might enquire into his condition it wouldn't be linked to the goings-on within the club. It was not only individual drug sellers who had to pay attention to safety in terms of detection; nightclubs also had to be careful not to be identified as places of illegal drugs activity.

There was also a resident dealer system in operation in the commercial London nightclub that Colin worked in between 1994 and 1998. This worked in a way where it was organised by the management and a handful of dealers were allowed into the club to sell. In describing the set up Colin said: 'The club has known dealers who pay a £200 payment for the privilege. The coke dealers pay more £400 to £500. I reckon the dealers sell 500 tabs of E a night and a lot of cocaine'.

One benefit to nightclubs in having resident dealers was drugs quality control. Club management could be assured, to some degree, that decent quality drugs were being sold. Sellers with resident dealer status didn't sell poor quality pills – not if they wanted to hold on to their privileged and lucrative selling status. From a management position, no nightclub wanted clubbers experiencing ill effects from contaminated ecstasy tablets, and drugs quality couldn't be controlled if club managers opted for the free-for-all drug selling approach. Collapse in a club could mean calling the emergency services, plus being branded with a bad reputation. Clubs that gained negative reputations were threatened with closure and some were closed down.

Club Dealers

Another type of nightclub seller was the independent moving seller. I refer to these as 'club dealers'. They simply turned up at nightclubs and dance parties with whatever drugs they planned to sell. This was usually ecstasy, though sometimes this included speed and cocaine too. This was a highly risky form of drug selling and for safety reasons was a style most of the dealers I got to know distanced themselves from. Anonymous club dealers were also the type of seller most people avoided having to buy from, unless you'd got to know them from a previous nightclub purchasing occasion. There was a high potential for being sold something resembling an ecstasy tablet, when it was no more than a paracetemol, from this type of club dealer. Most clubbers I spoke to over the course of my observations, either had themselves, or had a friend, who'd been ripped off by a club dealer, paying £10 or £15 for an ecstasy tablet that turned out to have no effect.

For those who were operating as club dealers, a key concern was not being caught by the club security, though even more important was not to sell to an undercover police officer. As the whole rave club scene stepped up a gear, methods of surveillance became more and more sophisticated. Undercover police officers dressed up as clubbers and operated in certain central London nightclubs. These worked in a similar way to that of the Lush minders, where on identifying people who seemed as if they might be selling, the tactic was to pose as a legitimate customer in the hope the person would reveal themselves as such (Jauch 1997).

Pamela and her boyfriend Ian were a couple I came to know who worked as club dealers. I met them through my attendance at Tylers club nights from the late months of 1994. They sold in a range of venues including high profile commercial nightclubs such as Club London, and in more discreet small venue clubs like Tylers. They merely turned up with a bag of ecstasy tablets to sell. It was from my observations of their club selling in action at the Tylers parties over an eighteen-month period, and talking to them more intimately, that I learned about their dealing operation.

They can be considered one of the random, unattached contacts I linked in with over the course of my field observations. Although they did join a chill-out session with Andy's expanding group in the early hours of one morning after a Tylers party, they didn't become attached to the group in the form of friendship. Friends could be made overnight in clubs, but Pamela and Ian's drug use was that bit too excessive for this group's comfort. Instead they kept them as club acquaintances and as useful drugs contacts.

Pamela and Ian were in their early 20s when I met them, and for two years had been driving into London from Essex on the weekends to sell ecstasy tablets in different nightclubs. Both were heavy ecstasy users themselves, and drank serious amounts of alcohol. Neither Pamela nor Ian had jobs. Drug selling was their job. They'd left school at young ages, and since then hadn't acquired any formal skills or qualifications. With their limited earning potential, drug selling was a useful, but risky alternative.

They researched in the usual way those going to clubs did, to work out which would be the best ones to sell at on that occasion. They did this by scouring listing magazines and picking up advertising flyers in shops. Sometimes they covered two clubs in the one night. It was well known that certain DJs and club nights attracted more hardened drug-using crowds than others, and techno-music clubs were known to attract heavy ecstasy users. These were the clubs that Pamela and Ian targeted to sell in. They were guaranteed profitable selling sites.

Club dealers avoided turning up at clubs with resident dealer systems in place like Lush. In these clubs, in a bid to protect the selling rights of the assigned resident dealers, the chances of being filtered out on the door, or by the roaming security inside, was high. Being caught usually meant having your drugs confiscated, plus being turned away from the club. Having drugs taken away was an expensive business especially in the amounts Pamela and Ian carried. They mostly took 100 ecstasy tablets along to a club. They paid up front for them at £6.50 a tablet, so confiscations could be costly errors.

There were few rules around the club dealer style of selling. No one person had rights to sell over and above anyone else. It was purely down to sales tactics and how you pitched yourself. Competition was fierce. In some clubs there were upwards of ten sellers at the same time. Pamela and Ian were advantaged here. Pamela stood out because she was a woman. Few front-line club sellers were women, and she was often recognised from previous selling occasions.

It was difficult for club dealers to disguise themselves. The very nature of their business was to promote themselves as ecstasy sellers, either by looking obvious, or by more blatantly advertising their wares. Some dealers reeled off the list of drugs they had available – 'Es, charlie, speed', as you walked past them. Club dealers were also obvious by their appearance. They were usually hardened drug users and were conspicuous by their sallow, drug-worn demeanours. Pamela and Ian stood out for this. They were young, but the years of living by night, lingering in dark corners of clubs, pepped up with alcohol and ecstasy tablets had taken its toll on them.

Pamela and Ian usually sold all the tablets they took along. At one chill-out session, Ian informed me they had sold 105 that night at the Tylers party. They sold at £10 a tablet, which was the going rate at this point. In purchasing at £6.50, they'd made a profit of £367.50 between them. Considering the distance they travelled and the level of risk they put themselves at, this wasn't a lot of money.

Aside from Pamela and Ian looking out for undercover police, the key safety strategy they employed while out selling in clubs was to divide the money and tablets up between the two of them, and the friends they were out with, if this happened to be the case. Being caught in possession of large amounts of cash in these settings was convincing evidence you were dealing, and the amount a person had on them could be the difference between a possession or a supply charge.

As it turned out, Pamela and Ian were in need of more rigorous safety strategies than they employed. One night in the mid months of 1996 I was talking to Ian at a Tylers party. He'd recently been arrested in the car park of Club London and was waiting to hear whether the charge was 'possession with intent to supply'. Club London was often mentioned in the rave music press for the targeted police attention it was attracting in connection to the drug selling on the premises. Pamela and Ian had become examples of this attention. They had just completed their night's selling in the club and were on their way out to another club to enjoy the rest of the evening. Ian explained the scenario:

> I had £900 cash on me and two ounces of puff. She had nine
> pills on her. She managed to stash them in the bumper of a
> car. We'd sold 90 pills. We'd just finished working. We were
> going on to another club to enjoy ourselves. Usually we make
> sure the money and pills are divided between a few of us,
> but it was just us. We were planning to spend £200 each on
> ourselves from what we'd made. We haven't spent any money
> for ages.

He'd been taken to the police station for questioning and not released until 2.00 pm the following day. While he was being questioned further police searches were carried out at his grandmother's house, where he lived, and an additional £450 in cash was found. Ian didn't seem ruffled by any of this. He said 'I've got a story up my sleeve. I can account for all the money. I want it to go to Crown Court, so there's a long time before the date. I'll plead guilty to the possession charge and tell them to drop the intent'.

The paradox was, at the same time he was relaying the story of arrest to me, he was busy selling ecstasy tablets to a stream of Tylers partygoers. Obviously, being caught hadn't deterred him.

Some weeks later I ran into Ian in a different London nightclub. He was still waiting to hear what the charge was in connection to the arrest, but he had received his summons to appear at the police station that coming week. He was somewhat anxious about whether it would be the more serious 'possession with intent to supply charge'. But for the time being, he was out clubbing and having fun and wasn't concerning himself with next week's events.

I didn't run into Pamela and Ian again in any of the clubs I was attending. Nitta did though. She'd become a member of Andy's growing group and through her regular attendance at the Tylers parties she'd also come to know them and saw them in a techno club a few months after I'd last seen them. She didn't enquire into Ian's legal case, but his presence in the club meant whatever the charge, he'd been spared prison. Again the irony was that he and Pamela were selling in the club. Perhaps selling drugs was the only way they could make a living.

Over the course of my field observations various people within the different social networks, as well as Pamela and Ian, came close to serious trouble with the law in connection to possessing different amounts of ecstasy tablets and/or cocaine. This was a drugs culture which was largely described as recreational, with few problems attached (Hammersley *et al.* 2002). This definition, though, largely concentrated on the health consequences of dance drugs use. Being caught in possession of amounts of drugs was mostly ignored but it was a hazardous side to participation, from which the legal repercussions could be long-lasting and detrimental. This was the fate of a few of the people in the social networks I socialised among.

Nightclub drug selling of the nature described with Ronnie and Vince, and Pamela and Ian was highly risky and few people I came to know were prepared to do it. It was observed that those who were positioned in these roles represented the marginalised young people written about by Russell (1993). Ronnie and Vince, and Pamela and Ian displayed enterprise and entrepreneurship in the ways they'd devised to make money, but they were also disadvantaged young people with limited educations and opportunities to engage in other, legitimate, forms of employment. Selling drugs to clubbers functioned as a useful alternative.

Rex was someone who also operated as a club dealer, though he was more cautious with his selling than Pamela and Ian. Rex and his friends were linked to Robin's group, and at a particular point in the early months of 1997 they merged together to form one big group. This came about through the regular socialising at the Pace Bar and Venus Group parties. Rex preferred the sales opportunities that arose within the moving dance party scene such as the Venus Group parties, where security operations were less stringent and the crowd less anonymous than in the commercial nightclub arena. Rex also performed the role of social network supplier fulfilling numerous requests that came his way. He always had supplies of ecstasy tablets, speed, cocaine and cannabis, if not on him, close to hand. At the time I was socialising among this group through 1997 and 1998, Rex was selling in the region of 50 ecstasy tablets a week. He wasn't working. He received disability benefit from an earlier work-based injury and the revenue generated from his drug sales usefully boosted his benefit payments.

Earlier, I noted the professional stance Rex applied to his drug selling. He'd been selling for a number of years, and was well aware of the scale of risk involved in nightclub selling. He made careful assessments of which events and venues were safe to sell in. Even though Rex concentrated the bulk of his club selling at Venus Group parties, it was still vitally important to be careful. He had a particular strategy. He made his selling out at these parties a swift operation; over and done with in an hour or so.

Rex preferred to move the drugs out of his possession as quickly as possible. One way he achieved this was to be there at the start of the party before other sellers turned up. This was to pick up the purchases of the early party arrivals. There was a genuine belief among clubbers that it was essential to get to a club before dealers' supplies ran out. The situation in clubs was often that ecstasy supply exceeded demand and purchasing was easy, but it could also be the case that people were roaming around asking everyone and anyone if they had 'pills for sale?' The early panic buying was what Rex liked to pick up, and within an hour or two, he'd usually sold all the pills he'd gone along with. Rex generally took 50 to 70 ecstasy tablets along to a Venus Group party. Once they were sold he went on to join in with the crowd, himself taking ecstasy, drinking and celebrating his earnings. At this point Rex was buying ecstasy in amounts of 100 at a time and was paying £7 a tablet. He sold at £10 a tablet, meaning within a couple of hours of trading he'd earned himself between £150 and £210.

Another key safety strategy of Rex's was reserving his own drug taking until his selling was complete. Rex said it helped him keep focused on the job, but necessarily it helped keep his wits about him. In his mind, taking drugs while working hindered his ability to keep his actions discreet. What was also important was that taking drugs while on the job made the financial accounting more difficult. He says: 'If I'm off it, I give pills away and let people pay later. It gets a bit messy and I end up losing money'.

Other sellers were not as controlled as Rex in this regard. Club drugs dealers were very often committed ecstasy users and in high revelry club environments, there was a difficulty in separating business from pleasure. Robin verified the risk of giving away her supplies if she took drugs while working. She comments: '. . . I become over generous, I shout everybody . . . I try and avoid doing it once I have had a few lines [of cocaine], because I don't think logically, and I don't care what anyone says, nobody can think logically on it . . . sometimes I tune out a bit too much financially . . .'

Another rule of Rex's in relation to minimising the risk of being implicated as a dealer was as far as possible, 'to not transport drugs'. What he meant by this, was limiting the frequency with which he transported quantities of drugs across London, especially by car. This was through fear of being stopped by the police and being caught with his supply. Rex often bought ecstasy tablets in amounts of 100 at a time and careful arrangements had to be made to get these bulk orders from his dealer's house to his own, on the other side of London.

It was while transporting a bulk ecstasy purchase across London that Ben, another person I came to know, was pulled over by the police. I met Ben in early 1993 through my work as a drugs researcher. He was 25 and was a London-born Turkish Cypriot man. Ben was a keen participant in the gay rave club scene and was selling ecstasy, LSD and cannabis to other gay clubbers. In late 1993, Ben was stopped near central London for driving up a one-way street the wrong way. The car was searched and the 70 ecstasy tablets and three and a half ounces of cannabis he had on board were found. This led to Ben being charged with 'possession with intent to supply Class A drugs' and a Crown Court trial ten months later. Ben narrowly escaped prison, but suffered the inconvenience of being returned to live with his parents and serving a home curfew order while waiting for the trial, and following the trial he was sentenced to probation and a community penalty.

This was precisely what Rex was trying to avoid. Even though his selling operation required transporting drugs from his dealer's house to his own, and from his own home to the clubs and parties he sold in, as far as possible he encouraged others to take the risk for him, for instance by getting his dealer to deliver to him. Rex also operated in a partnership type arrangement with Robin, where they occasionally made bulk purchases of 200 and 300 ecstasy tablets; half for Robin and half for him. Shrewdly, if Rex could arrange it that Robin took the transportation risks, he wouldn't offer otherwise. Of the six key characters I focus on for their role in drug selling, Rex was the most clinical and premeditated of them, who in ensuring his own personal safety, persuaded others to take risks on his behalf. There was a large degree of camaraderie among clubbers and their drugs contacts, but exploitation and functionality also underpinned social relations.

One thing that made this easier for Rex was the naivety of some of the people he was socialising among. This was the case with Ned. Ned was a young member of Robin's friendship group. Ned was 21. In the same way as Robin, he'd come over from Australia to spend time living and working in London. He found the whole London rave club scene super exciting and he was regularly out clubbing and taking Es. He was one of the members of Robin's group who frequently took five ecstasy tablets on a night out. Plus, he was one who despite being completely 'out of it' and an embarrassment to himself in terms of his physical state, was full of bravado about the large numbers he took. He was regularly gloating, 'Ah, I did five Es last night, it was wicked man, how many did you do?' Not long into his stay in London Ned ran into money problems. Rex read Ned's limited cash flow, plus his naivety, as a golden opportunity to offer him a role assisting in selling ecstasy tablets out among their friends, as well as shadowing him selling at Venus Group parties.

A few months earlier Ned's exposure to the rave club culture had been close to non-existent and his understanding of selling drugs in public places even less. With this lack of awareness, he was ignorant as to the level of risk he was exposing himself to. Ned was fortunate to come through his involvement in selling without being caught, but it was probably his decision to get on the plane and prematurely return to Australia later in 1997 that saved his skin. The clever way

Rex had crafted Ned's role, combined with the blurring effects of Ned's heavy ecstasy use, meant the high level of risk he had put himself at hadn't even registered.

Opportunistic sellers

The third type of club seller was the opportunistic seller. Opportunistic sellers were people who, every now and then, sold small quantities of drugs in clubs. This generally came about when a friendship group purchase had been made, and some of the purchase ended up as surplus to requirement, though it also occurred as people deliberately purchased extra tablets with the intention of profiting from this selling style. Indeed, it was often done to pay for the cost of the night out. Going out clubbing wasn't a cheap pastime. A night out could easily cost upwards of £60 once the club entry fee, drugs and alcohol expenditure, and taxis home had been taken into account. As an every now and then excursion it was manageable, but for many of the people I came to know, going out clubbing was a weekly pastime. If costs could be kept down by selling a few ecstasy tablets out in a club, then those positioned to do so, took the opportunity. This style of selling carried the same risks as that relating to club dealers. The only difference was opportunistic sellers had smaller quantities of drugs in their possession, and were not quite the same target for law enforcement as club dealers. Simon was an opportunistic seller.

Simon was aged 22. I met him and his friendship group at Tylers two years into my field observations in 1995, and for an eighteen-month period they became members of Andy's friendship group formation. They were frequent attenders of the Tylers parties and I socialised alongside them at these club nights as well as in more intimate friendship group gatherings from where I observed their purchasing and selling arrangements.

Simon's group lived outside London in a busy university town and regularly travelled in for nights' out clubbing. This was a small clique of friends and lovers; five in total, two of them were sisters and there were two couple relationships. They were moderate ecstasy, speed, cocaine and cannabis users. Simon and his girlfriend Ravinda were full-time students. Theirs was a relationship constantly under financial pressure. Both had incurred large debts due to general living expenses and an ongoing clubbing lifestyle. As a form of minor financial relief they often sold ecstasy tablets out in the nightclubs they went to. Once the club selling technique had been learned, and more importantly been successful, the lure to try it again was hard to resist.

On one of the nights I was out clubbing with Simon, Ravinda and the wider friendship circle, Simon sold sixteen ecstasy pills. This was at a small venue club night in south London. Simon took twenty tablets along on the off-chance he would sell a few. You could never be sure how thorough the security would be in smaller nightclubs. It tended to be less rigorous than in commercial clubs, but some clubs were located in high visibility areas and put concerted efforts into controlling the supply of drugs. At the same time the reality was that the success of a club night could be down to whether there was a drug supply available in the venue. This club was one that was well known for its rigorous checks on the door, plus roaming security inside. Pockets and bags were searched, but Simon got the tablets through in his underpants. This was the way male clubbers usually got their ecstasy pills past the door security.

Without effort, Simon sold virtually all the tablets he took along. At the end of the night he had one remaining. He and Ravinda had taken three between them, and the rest had been sold to anonymous purchasers asking to buy. The club was busy that night and although security roamed the floors keeping a check on trading, subtle tablet and cash exchanges were easily made among the closely packed dancing crowd. Simon was selling at £12 a tablet. He'd paid £8 each for them so £60 profit was made. This wasn't a huge amount, but eliminating his clubbing costs was welcome.

Simon and Ravinda certainly watched themselves in terms of avoiding being caught, but most attention was placed on the financial side of things. This was on not spending the money that had been paid out for the pills in the first place. Ravinda commented, 'It's easy for him to spend the money he's taking in, but we have to hold back what we've paid out for them'. Financial debt was one of the reasons they were selling in the first place, and they couldn't afford to mess it up.

Andy was also an occasional club seller. I refer to Andy as a busy mover since he was constantly latching on to the different revenue raising opportunities that existed within the rave club culture. In addition to being a low-level friendship group seller, he also made small amounts of money selling ecstasy tablets out in the clubs he went along to.

One of the occasions in which Andy sold out in a club was in early 1996 when he ended up with a surplus supply. Group purchases prior to going out clubbing were necessarily made by a person in the group who had access to a dealer, and Andy had this access. In setting himself up as a low-level seller, he made constant efforts to secure access, and at this point he was mainly relying on Joe's trustworthy supplies. The events leading to this nightclub selling occasion were that Andy had offered to purchase six ecstasy tablets on behalf of his work colleague. Since he was going out clubbing that night, and placing an order anyway, this wasn't putting him out. Andy was picking up half an ounce of 'hash' for his brother, three grams of speed for a friend he was going clubbing with, and four ecstasy tablets for himself. This was what a typical friendship group order of his looked like.

Andy arranged to meet Joe in a pub early on the Saturday evening to pick up the order. Joe often met with his customers in pubs across London. Pubs in London were easy exchange points. Alongside sitting with a beer and chatting, the drugs and money could easily be handed over. Publicans and pub staff rarely concerned themselves with subtle drugs activity, if indeed they noticed at all.

After the pub meeting, Andy went along to the London train station where he'd arranged to hand over the order. His colleague failed to turn up, leaving Andy with six ecstasy tablets he hadn't planned on having. More importantly it was leaving him £63 out of pocket. This was money Andy couldn't afford. On his low income he didn't have much money. As a solution, he took the tablets along to the club he was going to, and without trying, sold them in no time. This was the same club night that Simon sold his sixteen ecstasy tablets at. Due to the tight club security, there wasn't a club dealer on the premises in the style of Pamela and Ian that night and people were searching around for someone to buy from. Three different people bought seven tablets from Andy. The tablets were sold for £12 each, making him a small profit of £10.50. Although only small, the critical thing was he'd made back the money he'd paid out on his colleague's behalf.

Andy had subtle safety strategies in place whenever he sold out in a club. One was the passive selling style he used. He relied on being asked by people if he had any drugs to sell, rather than advertising he was selling. When anyone asked him if he 'had any pills to sell?', Andy responded 'Wait here, I'll go and see if he's got any'. In using this tactic, he made out he was getting the tablets from somebody else, instead of him being the person selling. In giving himself this time lapse, he believed he could work out whether the person was a genuine purchaser, or whether they were a part of the club security who were trying to flush out opportunistic sellers like himself.

The exchange was then done discreetly among the closely packed dancing club crowd.

An earlier occasion when Andy had ended up selling in a club was in 1995 when he had picked up an order of 40 'tabs' of LSD from Joe. With a bit of advance notice Joe could get most drugs his customers wanted. Andy had been asked by someone if he could get them twenty LSD tabs. Because of their cheap price, Andy decided to purchase twenty himself. Sooner rather than later he and his friends would consume them, or he'd easily sell them on. The demand for drugs within the rave culture was such that supplies were quickly shifted. Andy met Joe in a pub in the West End to exchange the LSD and money.

Andy was meeting friends to go clubbing immediately after meeting with Joe, and didn't have time to take the drugs home. The club they were going to was in the middle of the West End and clubs located in these high visibility areas came under greater scrutiny than clubs that were slightly off the beaten track. As it turned out, this club had recently had a visit from the 'club squad,'[1] who at the height of the rave club culture were extremely rigorous in their monitoring of drug selling in nightclubs, particularly West End ones (Ward and Fitch 1997: 120). Despite the checking of bags and pockets on the door Andy got through without the LSD tabs being discovered. He hadn't even contemplated selling them in the club, mainly because it wasn't considered a club drug. But, because of the tight security there was no drug supply in the club and Andy was being asked by people if he knew 'anyone who's selling?' This was a common mantra heard in clubs as people trawled around trying to seek out who was a source of supply. Not expecting anyone to take up the offer, Andy offered the LSD and ended up selling four for £5 each. He'd purchased them at £1.85 a tab, which gave him the small, but welcome profit of £12.60. These small amounts were all additions to Andy's low earnings and helped fund his club drug lifestyle.

Opportunistic club drug selling was very different to the other two nightclub selling roles. It was small-scale in nature and the transition to engage at the level of resident dealer, or club dealer was a big leap to make, and one the majority of opportunistic sellers simply didn't contemplate.

Andy and Joe as organisers of club selling

An interesting example to finish off these illustrations of nightclub drugs dealing is how Andy, Joe and Robin's boyfriend, Nathan, came together to construct their own club night and in turn create a dealer role; a role that yielded generous profits. Moreover, this type of club night organisation demonstrates the entrepreneurship of some rave participants. It wasn't just commercial leisure entrepreneurs in the form of the Tylers couple, or Tom and his friend who were setting up innovative and popular club style events, many rave club participants got involved and were contributing to shaping the burgeoning drugs use culture and economy underpinning the rave club scene.

In the beginning, Andy and Joe's relationship could be interpreted as a functional one. Andy was keen to secure access to a dealer to assist the low-level dealer role he had positioned himself in, and Joe made money out of the extra people buying his drugs. At this early point, not a lot else supported the relationship. As time passed, Andy and Joe became good friends who regularly socialised together, and went on to do business together in organising a series of club nights.

Organising a club night wasn't difficult. All it required was finding a venue, booking it for a night, attaching a name to the event and beginning to market it among the friends you knew. This was exactly what Joe, Andy and Nathan did. Andy had some prior experience with this. He and Colin had organised a club night earlier in 1994. This was in the venue the Lush nights were held in after Lush moved to a different venue in north London. It hadn't been quite the success they'd hoped in terms of attendance, but on this later occasion they didn't see how it could fail. Between the three of them they knew a lot of people who would come, they all had reasonable DJ skills so the music was taken care of, and there was Joe's drug supply, combined with knowing people who were prepared to sell them.

From their clubbing experiences, they were very aware of needing an ecstasy pill supply on the night for it to be a success, and made it a central part of their planning. Even though Joe sold at the free-parties, and Andy engaged in opportunistic club selling, neither was prepared to sell at this event. They rationalised, 'We're gonna be speaking with the manager through the night. The attention'll be on us. We need to get someone to do it'. There was also caution because of the high-profile location of the venue. The point at which they were organising their club nights was later on in my fieldwork in 1998, and drinking venues in and around central London were turning themselves into mini-clubs. On certain nights of the week an entrance fee was charged and a club atmosphere was created. This was the type of venue these guys had chosen, and because of its high visibility location, serious care was needed in respect to drug selling.

On the first of their club nights, Robin and a friend of Joe's – Lee – agreed to sell. Robin often sold out at Venus Group parties, so was practised in what was needed. Plus, Andy had seen her out selling and felt comfortable putting the job in her hands. Lee was a member of Joe's free-party group, and although he had little experience with nightclub selling, he was friends with many of the people coming along and agreed to take it on.

To make the dealing task more attractive, Joe offered the ecstasy tablets on credit. Added to that, he was charging just £5 a tablet. This was in 1998 and by this point, through Andy's negotiations, Robin was getting her drug supplies from Joe and she said 'this is a cheaper rate than he's ever given them to me before'. The going rate for an ecstasy pill in a club at that stage was £10, so the two of them stood to make a decent profit. The club night was a great success. Lots of people came; the venue space was good and lots of ecstasy pills were sold. Robin sold twenty ecstasy tablets and seven one gram wraps of base speed, making a profit of £170. Lee sold in the region of 70 tablets, making a profit of £350.

There were endless club nights that Andy, Joe and Nathan's friends could go to on any night of the week where drugs could be purchased, but with Andy, Joe and Nathan organising this club night they were in on creating and perpetuating a context in which drugs would be taken among their friends while at the same time creating opportunities to make money through the door charges and drug sales. This type of club night organisation and drug using environment was going on across London and was an illustration of the enterprising ways in which the people were making sure they got a slice of the pie.

Summary

These different nightclub drugs enterprises are illustrations of the ways people were positioning themselves to take advantage of the money that could be made selling drugs within London rave clubs and dance parties. Nightclubs were ready-made, open marketplaces and large quantities of drugs could be sold. People operating in resident dealer and club dealer roles made considerable profits through their selling, but across the board, selling in these environments was a highly risky undertaking requiring intense planning and organisation, caution, discipline and steady nerves.

Aside from Rex, the small number of people I observed who were positioned in the much more risky role of commercial nightclub selling, such as Ronnie and Vince and Pamela and Ian, were to some extent people who were limited in their ability to participate in the legal economy. They were from low socio-economic and marginalised backgrounds and were restricted to unskilled, poorly-paid work. Nightclub drug selling acted as a useful substitute. For these people, it was highly plausible that occupying this role was not so much a choice as economic necessity.

The growth in the rave drugs economy provided useful openings for those who had the motivation and necessary contacts to enter. The money people could make through drug selling compared to that they could make through regular work kept them tied to the role.

The opportunistic seller was different. This was more about funding clubbing and drug taking lifestyles, than earning a living. Though any drug selling in high visibility clubs was risky and it was only those that needed money who did it.

These rave club drugs enterprises can also be seen as facilitated by the nature of the London urban context. London is a large city that was home to a thriving rave club scene. Multiple opportunities were available to conceal drugs market organisation and trading activities within the general urban bustle and people movement. Moreover, it was impossible for law enforcement authorities to monitor and police all rave leisure venues, and the drugs activity going on within them. People knew this and took advantage.

Note

1 The club squad was a colloquialism for the Eight Area, Clubs and Vice Unit; the specialist police unit enforcing licensing regulations in clubs and bars in the central London area. At the height of the rave club scene in the mid 1990s, the unit actively sought to disturb drug selling in central London nightclubs (Ward and Fitch 1997).

Chapter 5

Social network drug selling

The previous chapter has described drug selling and purchasing in London rave clubs and commercial dance parties. In this chapter drug selling among social network contacts is discussed.

In the same way drug selling enterprises located in nightclubs and dance parties could become quickly established, social network styles of selling could accelerate rapidly and often beyond what a person had originally intended. Social network selling typically occurred in a drift-like fashion as friends, and friends of friends looked to purchase from whoever had a reliable and quality supply. In this way they comprised small and larger-sized operations. In this chapter I am focusing on people who were running larger, more commercial style enterprises. This was where drugs were purchased in bulk amounts to supply an established customer base, and considerable profits were made.

Generally social network dealers took a more cautious approach to their selling than those who sold in clubs. For the most part sales were concentrated among friends and known contacts, and were restricted to prearranged deals carried out in disguised locations. Social network dealers set themselves apart from nightclub dealers and were often heard defending their selling based on the fact they didn't sell anonymously in clubs. In their view the type of selling they engaged in, responded to the demand for drugs rather than created it. They simply saw themselves as providing for friends' drug needs. In contrast, club-based selling was viewed as high risk and was not a style many people I came to know were comfortable to engage in. Robin, who for the most part was a social network seller, expresses her sentiments on nightclub selling – 'I won't just go straight into a club and sell drugs, cold calling, that is just stupid and that is just asking for it'.

A key safety strategy for all dealers was keeping a low profile and anonymous selling in commercial rave clubs was considered high risk.

Even though social network dealing was considered to be a less risky selling style it was still dangerous and vital safety strategies were observed in order for dealers not to be caught. A range of tactics were in place to lessen the risks. A common one was restricting the numbers of people who had access to them. This was generally achieved through selling larger quantities to smaller numbers of people, who then sold on to others through lower-level dealing arrangements. There were also expectations on purchasers to assist in keeping activities discreet.

It is difficult to situate social network dealers precisely in the private domain, as although many of them had intentions to keep their selling confined to friend and social network sales, opportunities to sell out in the public domain were sometimes taken. Robin claimed she didn't take part in 'cold call' selling in nightclubs, though on a couple of occasions following bulk purchases of 100 and 200 ecstasy tablets, she did go along to a club to help shift them on – 'just for a few hours to get rid of some'.

Robin as a social network dealer

Robin was a social network dealer whose scale of operation fits that of a more commercial enterprise. Even though she sold out at dance parties, her selling style mostly comprised of supplying friends, and friends of friends with ecstasy, cocaine, speed and cannabis for their nights' out clubbing, and their more general drug-using lifestyles. She explains: 'It is just sort of a convenience network, people pass it all down to each other, and I would rather my friends getting good quality drugs and knowing what they are taking, than getting shit cut up stuff and wasting their money or possibly having a bad E . . . '.

Robin describes how her selling in London 'kind of just took off' alongside the number of people she was socialising with who were regularly looking to buy ecstasy tablets. She loved it. She was a party girl and the planning of nights out clubbing, and taking orders for ecstasy pills and other drugs from her Australasian network had her out there and in command. As well as feeling like her business simply took off, Robin alluded to social network sellers of her style being deliberate in the connections they looked to make with higher level dealers. This is to secure the necessary access to making 100 and 200 pill purchases to sell on to friends in smaller quantities:

> It took me a long time to get a constant, a reliable source to get drugs off, and someone who I could go and visit regularly . . . Once I found someone I could trust, I sort of hung on to him and I have been doing that for the last year and a half. Pretty continuous.

To provide for her social network's drug demand Robin regularly made purchases of 50, 100 and 200 tablets, and one deal she went in on with Rex in the early months of her selling was 300 tablets. These purchases were based on estimating the demand she would receive in line with the forthcoming party dates. Some sellers aimed to shift their supplies as soon as possible, but Robin wasn't bothered. She had a full-time job and with this had a regular income. The money she made from dealing was simply on top of her weekly earnings. At the peak of her selling through 1997 and 1998 she estimated she was selling 50 ecstasy tablets a fortnight, as well as amounts of speed, cannabis and sometimes cocaine.

The bulk of Robin's selling activity took place on the weekends as she sorted out friends' last minute drug orders in the run-up to the night out clubbing. Robin had a range of exchange styles in place. Sometimes she met people out in a local bar or pub prior to heading off to the club, or during the week Robin regularly drank at the Pace Bar and drugs were often exchanged there alongside a few casual drinks. Sometimes people came to her house to buy. Robin was advantaged with this. She lived in group housing set-ups, sharing with five other young people also living temporarily in London and enjoying the party vibe. The busy comings and goings of the shared household easily disguised the busy activity of her selling. One of the key requirements of social network selling is to keep it discreet and lots of person activity in and out of a private home is something that needs to be kept down. But Robin's frequent visitors just looked like lots of housemates coming and going.

Even though Robin's friendship group was one of high revelry and bravado, and drugs taking and purchasing among them was cavalier and often obvious, Robin had a range of tactics in place to protect herself from being caught. Firstly, she attempted to restrict her selling to people she knew, although there was the odd occasion when she turned up at commercial clubs with ecstasy tablets to sell to whoever wanted to buy. Robin explains her general approach: 'Keep it as low profile as I can and just do it to friends that I can trust. It actually gets a bit scary when you are dealing with people you don't know because the paranoia really kicks in'.

In line with the unwritten rules around dealer codes of conduct, there was particular caution in the way Robin interacted with the dealers she purchased from. Care was applied in phone communication when placing orders, although she did acknowledge they were a bit slack and thought they ought to be more vigilant:

> When I ring up and say what I want, we should be a lot
> tighter. We have started saying 'same again of either E or S' or
> whatever code. E for ecstasy, S for speed, C for coke or green
> or black – hash, marijuana sort of stuff, but we really should
> be a lot more tighter.

There were also unwritten rules about where and how her bulk supplies of 100 were exchanged and the money owed for them, and Robin particularly commented on the arrangements surrounding pick-ups from her dealers. These are the riskiest points of dealers' tasks. This is the moment when a large quantity is being carried, and the handover is a point around which much anxiety is expressed:

> The whole exchange thing, just carrying it on me, once I have
> got it in to my house and it is hidden I am fine, but it is when
> I am actually carrying a number of pills, even when I go out
> just to a club and I am carrying five or six on me I freak out.

The dealer Robin was using at this point when she was discussing handovers didn't like serving her from his house. This was due to his attempts to keep the number of people coming in and out down. Social network dealers attempt to limit the number of people they allow to collect orders from their home. An obvious sign of a dealer's residence is streams of people coming and going for short periods of time. To avoid this, locations in which drugs are exchanged are routinely varied. This includes selling from their home on some occasions, and meeting people out in public places such as pubs and bars, on others. Different public places were used by Robin and her dealer.

She describes the situation that exists between her and her dealer in regard to drugs exchanges. Her comment also illustrates the functional nature of the dealer–customer relationship. It is apparent, at this point she doesn't know him particularly well and in this situation security issues become even more paramount:

> Personally I would rather go to a pub or meet him somewhere else, definitely, because I really don't know enough about this guy. I have known him ever since I have been in England for two years. I have never seen him in any trouble, but who am I to know who he deals with and whether they are monitoring him, or the people he deals to or any of his friends, but I know he has got a lot of dodgy connections.

Robin was also using the unique and rather risky opportunity presented by using the motorbike courier service of the banking institution she worked in, to dispatch money to her dealer, as well as the occasional drug drop-off to her customers: '. . . I am lazy about going back up there again, I will send it in a courier. It is just easier, less fucking around, less people hanging out the front of his house sort of stuff.'

A common observation made among the people I got to know who were social network dealers was that at a certain point the enjoyment of the drug selling and drug taking lifestyle began to diminish. Personal health issues were emerging in connection to the ongoing use of ecstasy and cocaine that seemed to come with the job. Plus, the increasing level of risk being encountered alongside the expanding numbers of customers had to be considered. This was the case with Robin. She was beginning to tire of the full-on clubbing lifestyle, her relationship with Nathan had ended and she remembered the previous period of her drugs excesses that she wasn't keen to repeat. She says: 'I went silly on drugs years ago and they fucked me up a little bit, panic attacks and all that and I just don't want to go down the same track, so I am very disciplined with my drug taking really'.

Joe as an example of a social network dealer

Joe is also a typical example of a social network drugs dealer. It was through the friendship that Andy and Joe formed from mid 1994 that I also came to know Joe. For a period of three years I socialised intermittently alongside him and his large free-party group. This was out at various social gatherings in pubs and bars, at a few Trash parties and around at people's houses where the unique features of Joe's busy and sometimes chaotic selling operation was observed and discussed.

Joe was introduced to the rave club scene in 1993 at age 20, when studying at university. He was already selling cannabis to fellow students, but alongside his entry into the clubbing lifestyle, his selling escalated to cover a range of drugs – and to a growing number of friends and random other people. The increasing numbers Joe was selling to was in part connected to the branch of the rave scene he socialised within. Joe was in the free-party scene and this scene was based on a collective type ideology involved in political protest, with anti-capitalist sentiments. In support for its cause, free-party social networks were open-ended and large in number, and Joe's drug selling corresponded in a similarly open-ended and growing fashion. Joe loved partying and his participation in social network drugs dealing was really about having a good time. The money simply came along with it.

In a short time Joe was running a busy and lucrative selling operation. It was difficult to pinpoint precisely the moment it turned to a more commercial enterprise, but in mid 1994 around the time I met him, he pulled out of university for a year period to devote more time to it, plus the party lifestyle too. The exact size of Joe's operation was difficult to judge, but through the years Andy purchased from him, from 1994 to 1998, he was the personal supplier to his own large free-party network, plus he was supplying a regular customer base of upwards of ten individual purchasers who themselves sold on to others. Robin had become one of these purchasers, and she regularly bought ecstasy tablets from him in quantities of 50, as well as sizeable amounts of speed and cocaine. On one visit to Joe's house, Andy witnessed a single sale amounting to 100 ecstasy tablets and the exchange of £500 in cash. At the time Robin was purchasing from Joe in 1998, she made a cursory assessment of the size of his selling operation: 'For him to be giving me good prices and for him to be giving me on tick when he is only working in . . . probably only earning £150 a week he has got to be dealing big quantities to be able to keep going and give me tick . . .'.

Joe purchased in bulk amounts each week, some of which was pre-ordered, and the rest was based on speculation as to how much he would shift over the course of the week. Joe was familiar with the drug use of his own free-party group. He'd partied with them regularly for months, and knew exactly the drugs they liked, and how much they got through over the course of a weekend's partying. The remainder of the order was guesswork, but as long as he had a plentiful supply of ecstasy, speed, cannabis and cocaine, he had most covered. Ketamine, LSD and temazepam could also be obliged, but pre-ordering was generally required. Not all of this was shifted in a week, but for Joe sitting on an excess for a while wasn't a problem. The rate at which he sold drugs meant that sooner or later they'd be sold. Joe purchased ecstasy in 100 tablet amounts, possibly 300 at a time. Cannabis was bought in 'nine bar' amounts (nine-ounce blocks). Base speed was also bought in nine bar amounts. This was the favourite drug of the free-party group. They each took a gram or two on a weekend out.

People who sold out in clubs often operated in partnership arrangements sharing tasks and responsibilities, but selling operations located in the private domain were typically run single-handedly with the host of tasks being juggled by the one person. This was the case with Joe. He ran his business on his own, and definitely had his hands full doing it. There were numerous phone calls, journeys to and from the dealer's house, deliveries to customers, weighing up, counting out and wrapping up drugs, generally keeping on top of the finances, and dealing with the customers he allowed along to his house to purchase. On one occasion after Andy had made a visit to Joe's to collect his supplies he said: 'the phone rang about 15 times in 10 minutes'.

All the tasks Joe was juggling required time and attention, but it was the individual orders he was fulfilling that were especially time-consuming. The free-party group wasn't a problem. They were religiously met up with in a pub on a Friday night prior to starting their weekend's partying. Their drugs were easily dealt out in the pub, and with the unique venues of Trash parties, it was easy to dole out drugs within the boarded up, disused buildings they partied in. It was the individual bulk order purchasers he was obliging that was the time-consuming bit. Some he let come to his house but care had to be taken with this. A key safety issue for social network dealers was limiting the flow of people into and out of their home. This is a sure way to raise suspicion and has often been mentioned in the literature as something social network dealers try to avoid (Waldorf et al. 1991). Joe tried to limit it, but with the numbers of people he was trying to satisfy it was becoming increasingly difficult. Some people he allowed to his home. The bigger sales were certainly restricted to being made from his house. Transporting large quantities of drugs and cash across London was risky, and was what most dealers tried to avoid. Even though Joe tried not to have groups of people congregate in his living room, according to Andy many of the trips he made up there to collect his supplies overlapped with a number of other people who were there doing the same thing. On one of the occasions Andy went to Joe's to pick up an order he'd placed, he said: 'His front room was full of people who he still had to serve. It would've taken ages. I left it. I'll go again tomorrow'.

Joe often asked his peripheral purchasers like Andy to meet him in the pub where he was gathering with his free-party group. Andy didn't often go out partying with the free-party group and these combined pub meetings assisted Joe to locate sales outside his home. Plus, they enabled him to supply a greater number of people than he safely could from his flat. In one swoop he could sell to upwards of ten people simply by arranging to be in a particular pub at a specific time. Pubs were easy environments for drug exchange, especially pubs with pool tables. People like Andy simply went along to the pub, had a couple of drinks and a few games of pool with the free-party people, and while at it, swapped money and drugs with Joe. The activity surrounding a game of pool made it easy to disguise the drug exchanges going on alongside it.

It was certainly the case that the nature of London as a large bustling city was helpful to social network sellers. Day and night people throng the streets, and pubs and bars are filled with drinkers, and in this way drug exchanges could easily be interwoven with normal social activity and daily life.

One of these Friday night pub-selling sessions was in December of 1996. I was there with Andy having a drink and playing pool with the group before they headed off on their weekend's partying. Joe served eight people in the space of an hour. A rough idea had been gleaned as to who would be there and what was wanted through phone calls he'd received during the week. As soon as he arrived at the pub the exchanges began and in the space of an hour Joe sold a total of 23 ecstasy tablets, seven grams of base speed, two grams of cocaine and around an ounce of cannabis.

As well as dealers applying various precautionary tactics around their selling, there were a number of ways they expected those purchasing from them to behave. The knock-on effect of one person being busted had the potential to seriously damage the lives of others, especially a dealer's who usually had a bulk amount of drugs stored in their home. An unspoken rule was not to pass on names to the police if you did happen to get caught. In these circumstances you were expected to claim that you'd purchased from an anonymous seller in a pub or club, and given that drugs were regularly purchased from unknown dealers in London clubs, pubs and bars, this was a perfectly feasible explanation. This was the tactic Jamie knew to opt for when he was caught by the police in possession of ten ecstasy tablets and seven grams of speed outside a pub in central London in 1998.

Jamie was a member of Joe's free-party group. He himself was a low-level dealer and one Friday night having just made one of his routine purchases, he was caught by the police while in the process of exchanging an ecstasy tablet with his friend. On being asked who had supplied the drugs, Jamie knew not to give Joe's name. Instead he claimed he'd bought them from an anonymous seller in the pub. This backfired. For Jamie to improve his chances of receiving a lesser penalty, the police pressurised him to return with them to the pub on forthcoming Friday nights. This was with the aim of identifying the person who had sold to him and was an illustration of some of the frustrations the police were faced with in their attempts to control this widespread drugs market. It was essential that Joe was not incriminated within this course of events, but the consequences of the story Jamie had given the police, turned into a gruelling situation for him.

Without doubt Joe made money out of his selling, but he wasn't a 'hard-nosed' businessman and the money certainly wasn't evident in his lifestyle. Joe wasn't flash. He didn't follow fashion, rented a small flat with a friend, travelled on public transport and took only the occasional holiday. Joe could have made much more money, but the problem for him was he frequently sold ecstasy and speed to his friends at cost price, and on occasions even forgot to charge. This was a particular problem when he sold while out partying. Joe suffered increasing levels of personal drug use alongside his selling. He was a heavy ecstasy user and took speed frequently, as well as being a big drinker. The profits he was making were literally being swallowed up. On one occasion Joe commented 'I'm going to stop selling at the free-parties, I just end up giving away'.

Along with the more hectic nature of Joe's drugs dealing and his increasing use of different drugs, his overall reliability was becoming more and more erratic and those who bought from him were beginning to complain about him. His day was becoming later and later as he slept off the after-effects of the night before, people were finding it harder to contact him by phone to get their orders through, and he was continually late to appointments he'd made. His lateness especially was commented on as irritating. Many of the people who purchased from Joe considered him to be a friend whom they wanted to see socially, as well as to get their drugs. Usually by the time he arrived at the place he'd arranged to meet someone, the time set aside to have a beer and catch up was reduced down to just handing the drugs over before either he, or they had to leave. On one occasion Jamie commented, 'Joe's got really unreliable, he's always late. It'd be good to have a drink and catch up with him, but he's always late, sometimes by a couple of hours'.

Encounters like this began to change the dynamic between Joe and his friends, with him feeling more like he was 'just sorting people out', and his friends feeling like all they saw him for was to get drugs. Despite complaining about his increasing unreliability, most of them continued to use him as their dealer. Although his service was erratic he was still the cheapest person they could purchase from and his drugs were always of a high quality.

Throughout the four years in which I intermittently socialised with Joe and during which time he sold drugs, he never saw himself as a dealer. This was based on his view that he 'only sold to friends'. The concept of friends was an interesting one. Many of those who engaged in social network styles of selling perceived their customer base as friends, but on further investigation, friends often amounted to people who had been met on just a few occasions and with whom sellers had only loose connections. The camaraderie among participants of the rave club scene meant people considered even those they vaguely knew as constituting friends. In doing so, favours such as accessing drugs could be easily asked and sellers' perceptions of their own selling could be diluted.

This account of Joe's daily routine gives a flavour of the busy organisational nature of social network drug selling and the multiple meetings and tasks that accompany it, plus the 24-hour vigilance necessary alongside it. It was characters like Joe, though, who were not entirely cut out for the more detached, functional style required of the commercial drugs dealer, involving making people pay up, and separating business from pleasure. Friends were useful customers, but the blurring between social network partying and commercial trading could come to be a problem.

Mick as a social network dealer

Mick was also a social network dealer locating his drug selling in the private domain among friends and other semi-connected people.

Like Joe, Mick's selling had started out with cannabis, which he sold for some years before moving on to selling cocaine and ecstasy too. Mick was aged in his early 20s when I met him in 1997. Earlier he'd been enrolled on a degree course, but had pulled out. Since withdrawing he'd held a range of jobs, mainly in restaurants, and topped up his income with the proceeds from selling cannabis, and now cocaine and ecstasy too.

Mick made money out of his selling but it was observed of these social network dealers that this was revenue simply used to assist independent living and paying rent in the capital. They certainly didn't live lavish lifestyles, but it helped in limiting time spent in menial and low-paid jobs, plus it funded their own keen drugs appetites.

I got to know Mick through the Pace Bar. He and his friends regularly drank there and in the same way as Robin and Rex's group began overlapping, Mick's did too. Mick and his friends, though, were more on the periphery of the rave scene. They went to the occasional Venus Group party and drank at the Pace Bar, but they were devoted football supporters. This occupied them in a different way. They regularly drank as mates in traditional pubs in their local area, watching football on the big screens and livening up the outing with sniffing cocaine in the pub toilets. Wins were extra cause for cocaine-using celebrations. Mick joined in with them, but the nature of his business meant he needed to be visible out in places like the Pace Bar where clubbers congregated, and among Robin and Rex's friendship groups picking up on extra trade and useful contacts.

The particular point of Mick's selling I am writing about here was through 1997 and 1998. He was selling two kilos of cannabis a month. This was to a stream of regular big purchase customers; to people he knew through the Pace Bar, and to random others who cropped up here and there. On top of this he was selling grams of cocaine, mainly among his football friends, and the occasional burst of ecstasy selling was engaged in. The cannabis selling was his main business. On his calculations he made £600 profit a month from it. The money made from the cocaine sales merely kept him supplied in it. The ecstasy selling was more sporadic. Depending on mood, a decision would be made as to whether he would take on selling at a dance party or not, and on the occasions he did, he usually sold between 20 and 30 tablets. On one occasion he bought in an amount of ecstasy to sell at one of the annual summer festivals he was going to. He went along to the festival, but spent the time partying and taking ecstasy himself with his friends. He hadn't sold any of the supply he'd gone along with, meaning he was seriously out of pocket. On his return he commented, 'I've got to get rid of these, I'm seriously out of pocket, I paid up in advance and I need the money back'.

Those of his weekly big purchase customers who were not part of his social circle were invited to his flat to collect their purchases. His other customers were served wherever it was convenient. Some came to his home, which was often combined with social drinking and sometimes dinner; some others he served at his workplace. Mick worked as a cook in a local café and it was easy to get people to drop in there to pick up their order. Others were met with brief encounters in suitably safe but often public locations, such as in pubs and bars, and on one occasion in the aisle of a local supermarket. For safety purposes social network dealers varied the locations in which they exchanged drugs. As well as it being a deliberate safety precaution, it also reflected personal convenience. Social network drug selling was a time-consuming business and if exchanges could be reduced by combining them with socialising, it helped cut down the workload.

Like Joe, Mick didn't view himself as a dealer, instead describing what he was doing as 'buying in bulk for my friends'. It was observed of social network dealers like Mick, Robin and Joe, that the social aspect of it was thoroughly enjoyed. The nature of the business had them in daily contact with people they liked, and the socialising they designed their exchanges around, such as meeting up in pubs to watch football and in DJ bars where other young, stylish clubbers congregated, was cutting-edge leisure and great fun. One day Mick was rationalising his rather extraordinary existence of full-time socialising and drug selling and said – 'I like it, I meet nice people, I can lose the ones I don't like, but I've made some lovely friends out of it'.

As with Joe, at a certain point, Mick's own drug use began verging on habitual, and various attempts to bring it in line were being tried out. Mick was in a situation where he'd got used to the income he had from selling. He referred to it as 'easy money'. But it meant his whole reason for being at that time centred on drugs. Mick once commented, 'no-one ever rings me up unless they want something'. Plus, the regularity with which he was in the company of people where cocaine was being used was making it difficult for him to resist and was taking its toll even on a fit young man like him.

House parties as facilitators of social network drug selling

In my endeavour to shed more light on the nature and extent of social network drug selling within the rave club culture a unique style of social organising which facilitated extensions in sellers' drugs market base is worth highlighting. As the rave club culture grew, all sorts of social events and gatherings were being organised that provided a context favourable for partying and drug taking. These were being organised by leisure entrepreneurs such as Tom with the Venus Group parties, but also more informally by friendship groups themselves. One way I observed this was in the form of house parties that mimicked mini club nights and which were ideal environments for selling drugs. In the previous chapter I described the club nights that Andy, Joe and Robin's boyfriend Nathan went on to organise in 1998. These were initiated by the previous successful house parties they'd held that they then realised they could convert into lucrative commercial events. The first of these house parties was in March 1997.

By this point, through the Pace Bar and Venus Group parties, Andy, Robin and Nathan had become good friends and they decided they'd celebrate their birthdays with a joint house party. Nathan offered to host the party in his flat which wasn't large, but so far his neighbours hadn't complained about the early morning after parties they'd been holding around there. Around 70 people came along to the party. DJ turntables were set up in the corner and Andy and Nathan DJed at it. Robin and Rex sold ecstasy tablets at it. Drugs taking was similar to any club night, possibly even more intense. This really was private space. Providing the neighbours didn't complain about the thumping techno-music, there were few chances of being caught.

The crowd was made up of friends of the four of them, including Robin's Australasian friends who had voracious ecstasy appetites, plus various people from the Pace Bar. Rex had a busy night selling. He sold 65 ecstasy pills at the price of £10 a pill. He and Robin had gone in together on an order of 200 ecstasy tablets, which they purchased from Robin's dealer for £6 each. So in the few hours of the party Rex made a profit of £260. The party finished in the early hours of the morning, but continued the following day at the Pace Bar where Rex sold even more ecstasy tablets. Owing to the success of the party, a few months later Andy and Nathan held a Saturday afternoon/evening party in the garden at Nathan's place. This time Andy called upon Joe to sell at it. Joe sold 60 ecstasy tablets at £10 each, which, given he purchased at a rate of £3.50 per tablet, over the course of a few hours in the garden he had made a profit of £390. Based on the high quality of the ecstasy tablets Joe had been selling, a few days later Andy received an order from a girl he worked with who was at the party, for 40 ecstasy tablets which would be sold on to friends at her boyfriend's birthday party. Andy didn't handle this size of purchase but on checking with Joe it was all right, she was put into contact with Joe.

These are quite simply examples of the networked reality of this drugs market. Friends put friends in contact with useful people and social networks were sites of high drugs activity, and indeed sites of perpetuating the supply and demand of different dance drugs.

Holding house parties like this assisted in creating a drugs market. Of course people didn't have to take drugs, but social gatherings with a clubby vibe, the techno-music to go with it, and a dealer in the corner with a bag of quality ecstasy tablets for sale encouraged demand and in this way it could be said that rave club participants were involved in creating the culture and economy of which they were a part. The economy on these occasions was the revenue from the drug sales.

Few of the social network dealers I came to know accepted being identified as a dealer, despite being engaged in full-time selling operations from which they made substantial amounts of money. This was largely linked to the stigma attached to the label. To Joe, the notion of a dealer had negative connotations and carried shame. At a particular point in my fieldwork when I was seeking clarity from Joe around his selling, he became defensive saying, 'You're making me feel like a dealer'. This applied to others as well. Mick defended his drug selling activities as 'I buy in bulk for my friends'. On closer examination of his supply network a number of people could be classed as close friends, yet a proportion were people he only vaguely knew. Further, providing friends with something they wanted was seen as a simple supply and demand equation and led sellers to rationalise their activity in another way. For example, the buyer was viewed as, as guilty as the seller. It was they who were choosing to consume illegal substances, rather than drugs being forced upon them by the seller. Indeed the loose perception of friends that existed within rave club drug selling enabled people to view their selling roles in a different light. Viewing customers as friends functioned to dilute the illegality of the activity.

The dealer identity was rejected by some, yet others took it on with enthusiasm. Prestige and status could be gained. Young (1971), in his theoretical writing on drug takers noted the status that young people could derive from drugs dealing. He argued this was particularly the case for young people, as the usual life avenues in which status is achieved such as meaningful employment or acquiring material status objects had not yet been opened up to them.

Summary

This chapter has provided examples of social network drugs dealing and the nuanced activity that surrounded peoples' operations. It has emphasised the unconscious and drift-like manner in which businesses became established alongside the busy demand for drugs within this leisure culture. What has also been emphasised is the highly networked reality of this drugs market as social and friendship networks were key sites of much linking and convenient associations. Useful drugs contacts were sought after and sellers and buyers alike assisted in connecting with opportune and profitable drugs trading contacts. The rave club scene was underpinned by a high level of camaraderie but the very nature of the drugs trade meant that friendship networks often included people with only loose attachments, and relations could sometimes be instrumental and functional economic ones.

Chapter 6

The role of women in drug selling

> As with previous youth cultures, women within rave tend
> not to be located at the levels of music production, event
> organization, drug distribution and hence profit-making.
> These are predominately male sites of experience. (Pini 1997:
> 153)

This chapter focuses specifically on the way women were involved in drugs dealing within the rave club culture. Without doubt, the bulk of 'front-line' drug selling activity in clubs, dance parties, and among social networks was carried out by men. Women though were involved; occupying a variety of positions and carrying out a range of tasks. Women tended towards lesser roles, yet I met a few who were in a front-line position and who were running busy, high-profile enterprises. A second more common way women were involved was in assisting roles, taking part in practical organisational arrangements both in nightclubs and among friendship network sales. A third position was the free recipient type position. This was women who were located close to a drug supply, either through a boyfriend or male friends, and benefited from it either in drugs or money, or both. Also in this chapter is a brief discussion of the way women tired of their partner's involvement in drug selling, and rejected and moved away from drug selling partners.

It is generally assumed that the purchasing and selling of illegal drugs is a male occupation (Rosenbaum 1981; Adler 1985; Taylor

1993; Dunlap *et al.* 1994; Maher and Daly 1996; Maher 1997; Davis *et al.* 2005). Women have typically been portrayed as occupying passive, victim roles, drawn into drugs through their male partners and, in the main, as depending on men to provide drugs for them. There is, though, a more recent research base, largely from the USA and Australia, which illustrates women as active agents who not only take charge in seeking out their own drugs, but who also run successful and lucrative drug selling businesses (Taylor 1993; Dunlap *et al.* 1994; Fagan 1995; Denton and O'Malley 1999; Denton 2001). The aforementioned research argues that the notion that women occupied peripheral roles, was generated from earlier drug eras, such as the heroin age of the 1970s and the crack cocaine market of the 1980s. These were different drug markets to those emerging with the widespread recreational drugs markets of powder cocaine in the 1980s (Williams 1989; Dunlap *et al.* 1994; Fagan 1994, 1995), and dance drugs in the 1990s and into the new millennium.

Similarly, Denton and O'Malley (1999) argued that the commonly held view of women being located on the bottom rung of the ladder in the drugs economy is because of the tendency for research to focus on 'subordinated users' such as those who are severely heroin or crack cocaine addicted. To provide a different view, their research focused on women who were 'successful dealers' and they argued that female attributes could assist in successful drug selling businesses. They noted the kin and socio-familial roles women are taught from young and how these 'soft-touch' traits could be beneficial in running drug selling businesses and in resolving conflicts.

There is limited literature referring to the role played by women in the buying and selling of drugs within the rave club culture. One exception is the work of Henderson (1993, 1999). From her study of young female participants, she noted earlier understandings of women's involvement didn't fit the style of the rave club culture. Henderson states women were not being 'frog marched into drug use by men and were not living unhappy lives as a result of their drug use' (1999: 41). From this, she affirmed that women are not in a 'passive victim role'. Henderson abserved women's place was more aligned to that pointed out by Pini (1997) in the quote at the beginning of this chapter. Women could be viewed as equal participants, but they didn't tend to be in entrepreneurial, profit-making positions such as selling drugs.

Similar findings were revealed from my observations. Despite women being present in nightclubs and at dance parties in large numbers, and consuming drugs in a similar fashion to their male counterparts, drug sellers were overwhelmingly men. Nightclub dealers were men, and at the lower level of the drug selling hierarchy, where smaller quantities of drugs were being bought and sold; men were generally at the centre of these transactions. Some women, though, competed in these roles and women definitely played a hands-on role in assisting drugs businesses and acquiring drugs for their own ends.

Women and front-line drug selling

It was obvious front-line drug selling was a position few women chose to occupy, yet I came across a handful who were located in this role. In the context of this book, a front-line drug seller can be conceived of, as someone who was at the centre of different drug transactions, was selling in a variety of venues and locations, and was shifting significant quantities of ecstasy and other drugs.

Pamela and Robin were two women I came to know who were positioned as front-line drugs dealers and who were both running their businesses in line with the general rules of the trade, and in the same firm and calculated style as the men I observed in these roles.

Pamela was the only woman who sold anonymously in clubs by way of being a club dealer. A few women were prepared to sell in a front-line position in the more intimate moving dance party scene, yet hardly any participated in 'cold call' selling in commercial nightclubs in the way Pamela did in Club London and at the Tylers parties.

Pamela worked in partnership with Ian. Their selling operation functioned in the same way as you would expect any joint business venture to operate. This was where the tasks were evenly divided, equal responsibilities were held and the proceeds were evenly split between them. Neither Pamela nor Ian had jobs. Both were reliant upon making the money from their club drug selling.

Inside the clubs Pamela was prominent in her role as a drug seller and stood her ground alongside both Ian and the other dealers present competing for trade. Club dealing was highly competitive. A number of sellers would be in a nightclub selling at the same time. Pamela put herself out there and got on with the job. This involved making it known to people she was selling, negotiating the sales, exchanging the drugs and taking care of the money she collected. She was popular as a woman seller. They were few in number.

This was the public side of Pamela and Ian's working. How the more private roles were organised was information I didn't manage to elicit. For example, I was curious whether some elements of the business were more oriented towards Ian's job, or whether all tasks were shared equally. I wondered how they arranged their bulk purchases prior to heading off to a club to sell. Pamela and Ian usually sold in the region of 100 tablets on a night's selling. Whether the riskier aspects of the business, such as collecting or receiving the bulk order was Ian's job, or either of theirs was not known. Or who took care of the finances?

It did seem some tasks were more oriented towards Ian. When Pamela and Ian were arrested outside Club London, Ian was the one who had the £900 cash on him, and, as a consequence, was the one who was taken to the police station and left with the drug charge hanging over his head. This may have been an indication that the holding, and transporting of the cash collected from the sales in nightclubs was his role, or an understanding between them, that if they were caught, it was better that one of them was, rather than both.

Robin is another example of a woman performing a front-line drugs dealer role. She bought bulk supplies of different dance drugs and cannabis to sell on to her friends. In a short time hers was a hectic business shifting 200 ecstasy tablets on average a month, plus speed, cocaine and cannabis. Robin had the right temperament for the job. She was bold, competitive and energetic. Another advantage was she had prior practice and knew the character types she was up against in the drugs world, not only customers trying to get cheap deals, but dealers who attempted to exploit her if possible.

Robin ran her business single-handedly. A few male friends occasionally assisted, such as her boyfriend Nathan and Rex, but in the main she ran the whole set-up on her own. This was from tapping into a supply in the first place to organising and setting up purchases, collecting orders from different dealers, and selling on to people in the various spaces she sold in. The same game rules applied to her as the men I came to know who were running front-line selling businesses, and similarly the same game rules were imposed by her in running her business.

It was also apparent that Robin was located at this level of drug selling for the same reason as the male dealers I came to know. She made money out of it, it eliminated the cost of her own frequent cannabis, speed, ecstasy and cocaine use, and status and popularity were also enjoyed. Drug sellers were popular people. The important role of the drug seller was recognised by rave club participants and large amounts of credibility were awarded to them.

In Robin's opinion it was easier for her as a drugs dealer than it was for men. This was because women are not as readily perceived to occupy these roles, and thereby less suspicion surrounds them. But she also considered her 'city image' of wearing a suit when she collected her supplies was a more convincing reason people didn't suspect her. Unlike the other key characters I focus on who could be defined as front-line sellers such as Joe, Rex and Mick, Robin ran her selling alongside the full-time job she held in the City of London.

> Girls, well especially with me, sometimes I feel a lot better
> when I go and pick up, especially if I am dressed in a suit.
> I feel a bit more discreet. Sometimes I walk down the street
> when I have just picked up and I am in a suit, and I am
> carrying all this stuff, and I feel like I don't stick out, I don't
> look like the typical dealer. I mean no one would ever suspect
> me of being a dealer at all because I am a professional really.
> I don't know, guys, I suppose you always class guys as a lot
> more dodgy.

Although, to some extent the front-line position didn't appear gender-specific in that these women were having to observe the same rules as men, and wouldn't have been successful in business if they'd adopted any other approach, the fact there were few women in this position must have said something about the job. Robin's view was that men are quite simply more inclined to take risks than women, but she also alludes to the possible need for physical defence in the murky world of drugs dealing, and admits she wouldn't be up to it if required:

> Actually I don't know any girl in London that deals. They
> are all guys. All the people that I deal with are all guys and
> I don't know why that is. It is not as if you are less likely
> to get done. If you're going to get done, you're going to get
> done. It doesn't matter if you are a girl or a guy. But guys
> are more likely to take risks than girls, definitely, but also if
> I got myself into trouble, I know I wouldn't be able to defend
> myself at all. I would just have to run.

Across the board Robin was operating in a man's world, from the larger scale purchases of 100 and 200 tablets she was setting up, to the sales she made out among friends and at dance parties. Aside from a couple of incidents where trust was compromised, she was comfortable in the role. She had lots of friends and received a lot of attention through the useful role she was seen to occupy.

Towards the end of her selling in London Robin experienced an encounter while trying to set up a purchase that she said had opened her eyes up to the riskier aspects of drug selling, and which had even put her off.

This was in 1998 and Robin was attempting to arrange a purchase of 50 ecstasy tablets. Through a contact at the Pace Bar, she'd been put on to someone who was operating higher up the drug selling hierarchy than she was used to. She didn't know him and he was also someone she described as having an edge about him in a way that some habitual cocaine users do. Instead of obliging her with the 50 tablets, he was pressurising her to buy 1,000 and she had found the whole experience especially unsettling. She describes how the discussions unfolded:

> I said this is what I am after and what can you do for me?
> And he didn't really like the fact that I only wanted to do 50s.
> He wanted me to do 1,000s . . . Okay, I don't want anything
> to do with it. He was quite forceful with me. And he really
> wanted to have a go and try and get me to take more, or see
> if I could get the money together to take more.
>
> He wanted money up front because he was going to get a
> really good deal on 1,000 but I didn't care because I didn't
> want 1,000. I don't want to come anywhere near that sort of
> shit, that is scary business to me, as far as I am concerned that
> is just messing with the big boys. So anyway he agreed that
> he would try and sort out 50 for me, and I said that I wanted
> to try one first so he went all right . . .

Robin described how she went for a quick drive around the block to exchange the tablet, plus the £10 he wanted for it, but her increasing unease with the situation quickly made her mind up that she wasn't going ahead with it.

On later reflection, she realised she'd been taking a serious risk in making even a cursory enquiry with this dealer. This incident illustrates the different dynamics and pressures people can come under at a higher level of the drugs hierarchy. Larger quantities of drugs are expected to be purchased, connections are often with unknown people, and deals are driven by money alone. The camaraderie of rave club participation gives way to the reality of the drugs trade, and the risk and exploitation that underpins it has a more edgy and threatening feel. Both male and female players are minded to learn how to protect themselves and this was a terrain Robin rapidly realised she wasn't prepared to step into: 'It turned me off actually, that's why I am sort of going through a bit of a no-go phase for a while, thinking, chill out a bit'.

Women as assistants in nightclub drug selling

Despite women being conspicuous by their absence as single operator front-line drug sellers, particularly in club selling, one position in which they were found was in an assisting role. Women located themselves at the side of male friends and boyfriends helping to operationalise drug transactions out in nightclubs and at dance parties. Women were just as keen clubbers and users of dance drugs as men. With the relative normalisation of this recreational drugs culture women were not afraid to draw on their skills and appeal to assist in profitable nights out selling in clubs. Typical roles I observed girls assisting in were as steerers and lookouts in clubs, in the way Colin did in Lush, as transporters helping boyfriends get ecstasy tablets past security into clubs, and as financial assistants in helping to keep drugs money in order.

The assisting role played by girlfriends and women more generally was an important one, although in some situations it was apparent the role wasn't gender-specific. The assisting role also occurred within male friendships. It was evident then that it was an important practical arrangement. In regard to selling in nightclubs, the woman's role centred more on safety issues, with the assistant functioning as a 'lookout', providing moral support and fulfilling useful jobs such as helping to hold on to cash or drug supplies. When it did become gender-specific was when domestic finances entered the frame.

Anna was someone I came to know who occasionally played an assisting role in her boyfriend Rick's ecstasy selling out in clubs. Rick's role as a drug seller was more that of a part-timer. Certain opportunities were latched on to, as and when they arose.

Anna and Rick were members of the large social network that

merged together out of the three friendship groups around the Pace Bar and Venus Group events. Through the years 1997 and 1998 my observations became progressively more focused on the drug use and selling activities occurring among this network. Both Anna and Rick were keen clubbers who went out and took ecstasy and cocaine most weekends. Anna was 22. She was sociable, attractive, and not short of male attention. She was white and had lived in London for five years, working in restaurants and bartending. Rick was also 22. He was mixed race, tall, charming, and also not short of female attention. He'd been born and brought up in London and at the time I am referring to here in the mid months of 1998, he didn't have a job. He claimed benefit and supplemented it selling drugs. He had the same money problems as other young clubbers I met living in London away from parents. The money needed to pay a market rent and to cover general living costs far exceeded what an unskilled young person could earn in a regular job. Rick hadn't got any formal job skills although he did comment on it being a pity that the useful and professional business skills he'd acquired through drug selling couldn't officially be taken into account. Rick says: 'If I could put the business skills down on my cv that I've got from drug selling, I'd have a decent cv. The organising it takes, managing the meetings with people and keeping the money in order, it's the same as running a business'.

Anna had been with Rick for a year at the point I refer to here. Since being together they'd lived a busy clubbing and drug-taking lifestyle. This had put pressure on their finances, but one solution they had improvised was going along to a club with a bag of ecstasy tablets to sell. By selecting the right clubs to sell in, a sizeable number could be sold and their financial stresses temporarily sorted out. This was more pressing for Rick, but Anna didn't mind helping out.

Rick and Anna's selling excursions operated in a way where a spur of the moment decision was made on whether the club night, or dance party they'd heard about, was a suitable one to sell at. This depended on a few things. Firstly, it was not being held in a high-profile central London location. They were not interested in that type of selling. Another consideration was that they themselves weren't eager to celebrate the event. They were on these selling excursions to make money, and mixing business with pleasure wasn't cost effective. It was easy for them to get into the party spirit and consume the drugs they were supposed to be selling. The occupational hazard of consuming the goods intended for sale has been comprehensively discussed by other drugs researchers (Waldorf 1993). Another important factor was that their friends wouldn't be at the party. This would also conflict with the intention of making money. Friends were likely to pressurise them to get ecstasy tablets at cheaper rates. Everyone knew buying ecstasy tablets in bulk meant they could be purchased for as little as £3, and the club price of £10 a tablet, especially if being charged by friends, wasn't a welcome one.

One selling excursion Rick and Anna had recently embarked upon was relayed to me by Rick one afternoon in the Pace Bar. They'd stocked up with a supply through his dealer friend. Rick was privileged here. He got the drugs on a sale or return arrangement. Sale or return, and credit arrangements were not something dealers entered into lightly, but he and Rick had been friends for a long time, and within authentic friend relationships, credit was sometimes extended (*cf.* Desroches 2005). Rick was rarely in a position to front an outlay, given he was doing this to cover his rent in the first place. Even though he was getting the pills at the reduced rate of £5 each, paying up front for a 50 tablet purchase would require £250, and this was money neither Rick nor Anna had.

Rick described the way he and Anna had worked selling in the club:

> We went along with 50 pills and sold them all, it was only a couple of hours. I was doing the selling and she was directing people over to me. We came away with a bag of money. You should've seen us, it was slick, we were like Bonnie and Clyde.

The 'steerer' role was one Anna often assumed. She had a few male friends who regularly sold ecstasy out in clubs and at dance parties and while out clubbing with them, often steered people looking to purchase towards her friends. Anna didn't comment on Rick and her selling session. She'd had a good night but viewed it as something that had to be done – 'Rick needed to pay his rent'.

Drug selling practicalities and assistance

Women also assisted in club drug sales in ways which incorporated the more hidden, practical aspects of selling, and work of this nature played an important part in the success of a night's selling. My observations of this subtle role were mostly within the opportunistic selling described in the previous chapter where small amounts such as ten and twenty ecstasy tablets were taken along to a nightclub in the expectation they could be sold. Women helped in various ways including getting ecstasy tablets into clubs, acting as lookouts, and helping to keep tabs on the finances.

In the earlier years of the rave club culture, before nightclub door security was tightened, people were rarely checked for drugs on entry to a club and women were checked to an even lesser degree. But, in line with legislation and stricter guidelines on the control of drugs in clubs, nightclubs employed both male and female door security to conduct searches. Searches weren't dissimilar to those carried out in airports. Uniformed staff frisked bodies and made people empty trouser and jacket pockets. Lots of chewing gum and 'rizla' cigarette rolling papers were confiscated, but it was difficult to detect drugs hidden away in underwear. Clubbers knew this and had devised tactics to use this to their advantage. Girls did favours for male friends and boyfriends by carrying drugs through for them.

Another particular way I observed girls assisting their boyfriends' selling in clubs was in a housekeeping-type role. This was keeping track of the number of ecstasy tablets sold and the amount of money being collected. I interpreted this as a form of 'holding the purse strings'. It was usually specific to couple relationships and was often bound up with domestic finances and financial problems.

A number of the people I socialised among were young and weren't working in well-paid jobs, or they were students. The expense of living in London, coupled with the cumulative costs of what, for many, were protracted clubbing lifestyles, had led to big debts that were difficult to reconcile. This was the scenario for Simon and Ravinda, hence Ravinda kept a close eye on the financial side of things when they were selling in clubs.

With Simon's high tolerance for ecstasy and a tendency towards greed in this respect, Ravinda kept a close eye on the number of tablets he was selling, the cash coming in, and the number he was consuming himself. Given they were engaging in this low-level club selling because of the financial pressures on them in the first place, it was essential the money they'd paid out for the tablets was recovered. As partial protection, Ravinda insisted on holding the cash on her person, thereby ensuring the outlay was held aside. She said: 'I hold the money on me. I know how much he's paid out to buy the pills in. That money's got to be made back, otherwise he's spent money that's meant to pay his share of the rent and food'.

Communication would be going on between them as to how much cash they'd collected through the sales and how much they could spend on their own luxuries whilst in the club – their own luxuries being the alcoholic drinks they could buy and the number of tablets they themselves could consume.

Assisting-type roles in clubs were not necessarily gender-specific but when domestic finances entered the frame, women played a discreet and important role in assisting their boyfriends keep on top of the financial calculations and staying out of drugs debt.

Women assisting in social network selling

Women not only assisted in selling drugs within nightclub spaces, they also performed assisting roles in social network selling. Drug transactions were mainly organised and carried out by men, but within both couple relationships and within social and friend networks, women were sometimes looked to, to help out. One typical way this occurred was women being called upon to utilise the drug contacts they had. In the same way as men made useful drug purchasing contacts as they went about their day-to-day business, women did too.

Charlotte was someone who had her own reliable drug contacts and who often found herself helping out. Her brother was an ecstasy seller and if people within the various friend groups she socialised among came up against obstacles with accessing supplies, Charlotte could assist. She didn't mind. She was just as keen to be using drugs on a night out as the rest of the group and all it required was a phone call, and a visit to her brother's place.

I came to know Charlotte in the earlier years of my field observations in 1994. A member of Andy's early group – Max – met her in a nightclub and they began going out. Along with Andy's group, Charlotte came out to different club nights and I became friendly with her over this time. In the way that clubbing networks overlapped, Andy's early group involving Charlotte occasionally overlapped with people in Joe's free-party group. From this, on breaking up with Max, Charlotte went on to form a relationship with Jamie. Jamie was introduced in the previous chapter.

Charlotte was aged 20 when I met her in 1994. She was shy, but very bright. She was in the second year of a medical degree. Charlotte born and raised in west London and lived at home with her parents. She came from a traditional working-class background, and her family held education in high regard. Jamie was older. He was 31 when they met. He was also bright. He'd studied at a good university and had an established career in the media. They both loved clubbing and loved taking drugs.

Prior to meeting Jamie, Charlotte regularly used her brother as a source of ecstasy pill supply. He always had top quality ecstasy and speed pills and he lived near her in west London. Since going out with Jamie, Charlotte had relied on him to sort out the weekend's drugs. But, there was a particular turning point when she found herself being looked to, to help out. This was when Jamie was arrested in possession of ten ecstasy tablets and seven grams of speed, as mentioned earlier.

Jamie himself could be defined as a low-level friendship group seller. He bought small amounts of ecstasy, speed and LSD from Joe and sold to different friends he knew. It was easy for the people who were in Joe's circle to take on a low-level selling role. This was due to the quantity of drugs Joe usually had in his possession and the ease with which twenty or so ecstasy tablets could be purchased from him.

Following his arrest Jamie quit his small-scale selling, but he wasn't about to stop partying and taking drugs. Instead, he simply turned to Charlotte to use her brother to provide the supplies. For a while she obliged, but it was around this time she was tiring of the drugs lifestyle, and it wasn't much later that they split up. It is examples like this where women can be seen as equally active in making sure the desired drugs for the night out were ready at hand. Girls also liked taking drugs, and it didn't matter who got hold of them, as long as someone did.

Colin found himself in a similar situation to Jamie in asking for drugs pick-up favours from his girlfriend Lisa. This was also following him being caught in possession – in this case of four grams of cocaine powder. Following the police stop, he quit the selling he was involved in, but also wasn't interested in quitting his drug use. He did cut down though. This was the point at which Colin's cocaine use was excessive and even though he wouldn't admit it, he was struggling to keep a handle on it. In attempting to avoid being caught again, Colin looked to someone else to access the ecstasy and cocaine that his small clique of friends used when they went out. It was at this point he looked to his girlfriend. Colin met Lisa through the London nightclub he worked in. She had a young child and also she had had a previous bad experience with a drug-using partner. She was seriously against the selling Colin was involved in, and at one point threatened to end their relationship if it continued. She enjoyed taking ecstasy and cocaine herself, but the selling side of it, in the way Colin was engaged, angered her. A while down the line when things had calmed down somewhat, Colin arranged it so that Lisa would collect from the seller's house rather than him. Since this involved fairly small quantities, and was on a relatively infrequent basis, she didn't mind helping out with the task.

Women obliging in the way that Charlotte and Lisa did was evidence that they too enjoyed the drug club lifestyle and if the main route of supply was down they would help out if necessary.

Women as free drug recipients

In contrast to the examples provided, where to varying degrees women took an active role in drug purchasing and selling, my observations revealed a position where women occupied a free recipient type position. This typically came about through being in a relationship with a drug selling partner. By default this located women close to a drug supply and meant they too reaped the benefits. It also came about as women deliberately positioned themselves close to male friends and boyfriends who had ready access to supplies. Nicky was someone whose boyfriend was a dealer and who got free drugs and money in this way.

Nicky was a member of Tom's group. I came to know Nicky through her socialising at the Pace Bar among the wider milieu of the large social network I became a part of through 1997 and 1998. She was a white Londoner aged in her early 30s and worked in the restaurant trade. She'd been living with her boyfriend Carl for six years. He was a similar age. He was also a Londoner. For as long as she'd been with him, he hadn't worked, and for the same length of time and longer, he'd sold drugs. Carl didn't socialise at the Pace Bar but he occasionally dropped by. Carl could be defined as a higher tier dealer. He sold cannabis and cocaine in sizeable quantities to just a few regular customers. To illustrate his level of operation, Carl was Mick's supplier and Mick bought half-kilo amounts of cannabis, plus about a quarter ounce of cocaine per week, and Mick was one of Carl's smaller customers. Carl's customers were those who themselves ran drug-selling businesses. According to Nicky, Carl had been in the drugs scene for years, not necessarily the rave drugs scene, just a drugs scene *per se.*

If you weren't aware of Carl's selling you wouldn't suspect him. His operation was highly discreet. Occasionally he sold at the parties of a dance party group, though this would be one where he knew the organisers, and it was usually them he was selling to anyway. Sometimes the occasional small sale was made outside of his regular customer base, but only when it was convenient, and only to someone he was familiar with. The sanctions are high if you are caught at this level of the selling hierarchy. Being caught possibly means a prison sentence, but it also means a change of lifestyle. Dealers at this level mostly rely wholly on the income they get from selling, so alternative work options can be slim. This was the case with Carl, plus, as Nicky says 'he's never had a job'. To make matters more precarious, his and Nicky's lifestyle had been brought in line with the amount of money being made from his sales. They weren't living a lavish existence, but their general household living and holidays were contributed to through his drugs money, and certainly their own voracious appetites for ecstasy, cocaine and cannabis were provided for.

The fewer people who knew about Carl's operation, the easier it was to keep it discreet. Nicky had no involvement aside from occasionally passing Carl's mobile phone number to people he was familiar with, or passing information on as to when he could be contacted. It was probable that Nicky didn't know much about his operation. This is a safety precaution. If Carl was unlucky enough to be caught, Nicky could claim she had no knowledge of what he was doing. Being able to distance herself from his selling became even more important following the birth of their child. One position I observed was women enjoyed the drugs their partners could provide, but there were real concerns when it encroached too much into the home, posing a threat to family life if they were to be caught.

Women as instrumental free-recipients

As well as women being in a position where by default they could profit from their partner's drug selling, there were women who deliberately positioned themselves close to a supply. These were women who consciously formed relationships and friendships with men who either had access to drugs through their role as a dealer, or were close to a source and were able to purchase it cheaply. This was especially observed around the supply of cocaine. Cocaine is an expensive drug, plus it is more likely for people to come to use it over a number of days per week, compared with drugs like ecstasy. Because of the particular physical effects of ecstasy, it was mainly a weekend club drug. As an indication of how common the scenario of girls knowingly linking themselves to men with cocaine became, the derogatory term 'coke bitch' emerged, and some men looked out for them. On one occasion down at the Pace Bar when I and another friend were sitting talking with Nicky, she was remembering the beginnings of her relationship with Carl and how he had been wary of her as potentially being one. Nicky said:

> Carl didn't trust me at first. He thought I was only interested in his coke. It'd happened before. Girls made out they were interested in a relationship with him, but it was only the coke they were after. He wouldn't sleep with me the first few times we were together. He was making sure I wasn't doing the same.

Through his dealing Carl was familiar with the practice of women who pretended to be interested romantically, when actually it was his cocaine they were interested in. It is important to note, though, that as much as girls knew they could use their sexuality to access drugs, men knew they could use their cocaine to access sex.

It wouldn't be fair to characterise Becky as deliberately positioning herself close to her male friends' cocaine supplies, but she was someone who frequently took cocaine, and rarely if ever paid for it. This was facilitated through her close friendships with various male friends and boyfriends who either sold cocaine, or were close to a cheap supply of it. Becky was also a member of Tom's older group, among whom she'd socialised since moving to London at age 19. This group's party lifestyle centred on cocaine-use. It was here Becky acquired a taste for it and had been using it on two or three days a week since. Becky was 23 and 24 at the point I came to know her through 1997 and 1998. She regularly drank with friends at the Pace Bar, and attended most of the Venus Group parties. She was popular and very attractive. She had lots of friends; male and female. Becky was usually in a committed relationship, but a pattern was established where more often than not it was a boyfriend who sold cocaine, or was closely connected to it. In the periods Becky wasn't in a relationship, there was a pool of male friends and ex-boyfriends she socialised with who to varying degrees were involved in selling cocaine. Becky's interest in these men fell into the category of normal friendship, and straightforward romantic relationships, yet it was my hunch the contact was sometimes initiated on the accessibility of free cocaine.

Women rejecting drug selling partners

It was observed that girls assisted their boyfriends with drug sales and collections, and used the drugs that came into the house, though it was also apparent there came a point when they tired of their boyfriend's involvement. Certainly, a number of long-term couples, I came to know through my socialising in these different friendship groups, split up during the time I knew them. Of course, relationship break-up occurs for numerous reasons, though a common cause among these people was the woman becoming fed up with her boyfriend's drug taking, or selling.

It was often the case that the clubbing and drug-taking lifestyle had been enjoyed together as a couple, and this was often the context in which they'd come together in the first place. It was observed, though, that for a number of women, there was a maximum threshold in regard to their partner's drugs participation. The tendency for increasing risks to be taken in respect to selling drugs, once someone had embarked upon it, such as buying in larger amounts and adopting a more cavalier style of drug use, put a number of couple relationships under pressure.

Rick and Anna were an example of this. A year or so on from the club-selling excursion described earlier, their relationship ended, compounded in part by Rick realising the ease with which he could make money from selling ecstasy and cocaine and becoming more and more involved.

This was also the case with Jamie and Charlotte. On occasions Charlotte assisted Jamie to acquire the weekend's drug supplies, but not for long. This was the point she began tiring of the constant drug use and partying lifestyle. They had been together for three years and the free-party style of socialising was intense. Charlotte was eager for success in her degree studies, plus Jamie was taking cocaine frequently and she was finding him a less respectful person for it. It was not long before they split up.

Lizzie and Jackson were another couple whose relationship went through testing times. This was connected to Jackson's increasing involvement in drug selling which was something Lizzie disapproved of intensely. Lizzie and Jackson were connected to Joe. They'd met at university in 1993. Initially Jackson and Lizzie had enjoyed a moderate style of clubbing and drug taking together, though Lizzie had since moved on from it, and was finding it more and more difficult to deal with Jackson's drift in the opposite direction. Jackson and Lizzie were aged 24 at the point I am referring to here in 1997. They'd met as university students four years earlier. Both were white, and from educated backgrounds. Jackson was training to be a medical doctor and Lizzie worked for a recruitment company.

Jackson had recently failed crucial qualifying exams, meaning his student status was to extend beyond the already long period it had so far been. This was a situation that was adding to his already huge debt. Jackson estimated 'I'm going to be about £28,000 in debt by the time I finish'. To alleviate some of the financial pressure he was under, Jackson fell into generating extra income through making the occasional large purchases of cocaine and ecstasy tablets and selling them to his fellow medical students. He was also every now and then taking care of Joe's drug-selling operation.

For a couple of years Jackson had been dabbling in selling small amounts of ecstasy, cocaine and cannabis. Lizzie had tolerated this, albeit through 'gritted teeth', but the larger amounts he was selling and the increasing frequency at which he was doing it, eventually fired Lizzie's anger. One of his purchases amounted to an ounce of cocaine and 60 ecstasy tablets for which he paid £1,000. From the purchase he said 'I'm going to more than triple my money'. It was not only the threat to his career should he get caught that concerned Lizzie, but the people activity within their flat connected to his selling infuriated her. Jackson was using their home to exchange the drugs. This was where Lizzie's resentment had especially built up. She expressed a particular anger at coming home from work 'to find people I've never met in my front room'.

Some women benefited from their partner's involvement in drug selling in that they too enjoyed using the drugs available to them at little or no cost. Lizzie, though, derived few benefits from Jackson's selling. Aside from smoking cannabis, she didn't take drugs. Some advantage to her lay in the fact that through the money Jackson was making he was not such a drain on the domestic purse. For some time Lizzie had been subsidising Jackson's contribution to the household budget, which up to a certain point she hadn't minded. She had long-term plans for their relationship and looked forward to the day when he would qualify as a doctor. Here she visualised a more relaxed life without the pressure of exams, and Jackson would finally be living off a doctor's salary. This wasn't to be. They parted company not far down the line.

Summary

What I have presented in this chapter illustrates the ways women were involved in the sale and purchase of drugs within the rave club culture. Through my observations it was generally noted that the purchasing and selling of ecstasy tablets, cocaine and other drugs was typically a male occupation. Indeed, the bulk of the front-line drug selling activities were carried out by men. Women, though, were involved, occupying a variety of positions and carrying out a range of tasks. This contrasts with some of the earlier writing on women's involvement in drugs markets, which located them in peripheral roles. It does though correspond with the more recent literature that emphasises their active and successful involvement. This female involvement can be linked to Fagan's (1995) assessment that social and recreational drugs markets created new openings and made it easier for women to take part.

Chapter 7

Scaling-up and moving out of drug selling

> People who were in it for fun in the beginning now saw it as
> a form of income. Either they were DJing, or running clubs,
> or they were selling drugs to the new initiates. The drug
> distribution system had stepped up a gear and it provided
> a way of living for and in the scene full-time; the £15 pills
> could finance a lifestyle of hedonism. (Collin 1997: 70)

This chapter focuses on the shifts and changes that occurred in peoples' drug selling set-ups. I look mainly at how drug selling activities increased over time as this was the overriding pattern I observed. The lengthy nature of my fieldwork gave me an insight into the way drug selling ultimately evolved. This was mostly as friendship networks grew in size, and the effortlessness at which drugs were bought and sold among them. It was easy to drift from selling a few ecstasy tablets at a time, to buying in bulk quantities, and looking for customers to sell on to. This chapter looks more closely at the context in which these shifts and increases occurred and some facilitating factors that lay behind them. Also included is a discussion of the scaling down of selling operations and people's attempts to move away from drug-selling lifestyles. It was evident that moving into drug selling was a relatively straightforward process, but exiting was proving difficult for some.

A theme drawn upon within the discussion of exiting drug selling is 'identity transformation'. It was apparent people were more easily able to draw away from drug selling lifestyles if they had an alternative identity to draw upon, or revert to, such as a return to legitimate employment and conventional work (Waldorf *et al.* 1991).

A number of commentators on drug distribution systems have discussed the way drug sellers make both upward and downward moves through the layers of the selling hierarchy, selling greater and lesser quantities of drugs at different time points and even quitting for a period, only to return to it again some time later (Adler 1985, 1992; Murphy *et al.* 1990; Waldorf *et al.* 1991; Waldorf 1993; Tunnell 1993; Curcione 1997; Pearson and Hobbs 2001; May *et al.* 2005). Murphy *et al.'s* study (1990) of entry routes into cocaine selling discusses upward shifts in people's drug-selling activities. They noted for the most part that people simply drifted into higher levels of selling from previous more novice styles of engagement. Similar drift scenarios were identified by Waldorf *et al.* (1991) in their study of heavy cocaine users. They noted the inevitability of moving into drug selling alongside a committed cocaine using lifestyle. This was usually to finance the cost of their own drug supply, but they also noted the status and prestige that was derived from it.

A drift type process was the way most of the people I came to know who were operating as drug sellers had come to be doing so. Shifts and increases in selling activity though also came about as conscious decisions to expand selling set-ups, usually on the realisation that significant amounts of money could be made.

Drug purchasing on behalf of friends

One typical way people saw expansions in their drug selling was through go-between styles of operation that involved purchasing ecstasy pills on behalf of their friends. For a large proportion of people the rave club culture was about having a good time out clubbing with friends, and a primary ingredient in this was taking ecstasy. It was apparent though that only certain people were able to access drug supplies and those people were looked to, to make sure they, and their friends had drugs for the intended night out. In this way, friendship group selling styles could easily accelerate to more frequent and larger purchases carrying greater risks. It was through purchasing on behalf of her Australasian network that Robin described the way the upwards shift in her selling had came about:

. . . all my mates were doing it and a lot of my close friends needed drug supplies and I sort of ended up picking up for them . . . I didn't and still don't consider myself now dealing . . . I'm really doing it as favours for friends . . . it's just sort of a convenience network, people pass it all down to each other, and I would rather my friends getting good quality drugs and knowing what they are taking . . .

Once underway Robin's selling increased month on month for the eighteen month period she was involved. Robin viewed herself as someone who could access ecstasy pills whereas others in her group couldn't. For some time she described her drug selling as 'doing favours for friends'.

It needs to be remembered though that access to a drug supply was often something that had taken careful negotiation over a period of time. For safety purposes, social network dealers restrict the number of people who have access to them, preferring to make larger sales to fewer numbers of people. From her previous selling experiences back in Australia, Robin was aware of this and for ease of accessibility to a 'reliable supply', she took the risk and made bulk purchases. Robin's bulk purchases of 50 to 200 ecstasy pills at a time were therefore connected to demand from her expanding group of clubbing friends, but also to the protocols of higher level dealers; limiting contact and favouring big purchases.

The link Robin made to a higher level dealer to make her purchase was a man she'd known back in Australia. He was an Englishman living out in Australia, but had returned to London and continued an involvement in drugs dealing back here. Robin comments on how she knew him, but also on the convenience aspect of buying larger quantities of ecstasy pills at a time. This example of Robin's networking in with a previous useful drug contact is a key example of the chain of contacts underpinning social network drugs markets. It can also be used to emphasise the nature of some drug relationships as purely based on economic gain:

He is quite a big boy. He used to actually drug smuggle into Australia and that is how I met him. He was my first contact when I first arrived here. But I had to go miles, to go and get it. It was like a mission so again that was also why I probably first started as well. Going that far, I wasn't going to go all that way just for 10 pills for one weekend sort of thing.

This go-between type of purchasing or purchasing on behalf of friends was responsible for others whose level of selling increased beyond what they had initially intended. This was how Andy's selling gradually shifted upwards, and as with Robin, led to his sustained involvement over a few years.

Andy was someone who drifted from selling small amounts of drugs to his friends, to a few years later selling ecstasy, speed, and later cocaine among different friendship networks. Andy moved from the relatively benign pursuit of drugs for his own consumption and his friends, to becoming a low-level friendship network supplier. Andy had a long history of clubbing and his earlier clubbing experiences started off in an environment of much less competition in regard to ecstasy supply. A supply of ecstasy in nightclubs at the point he started out in 1990 was much less of a guarantee than it was in later years, when there could be upwards of ten dealers in a club selling at the same time. Supplies for a night out definitely needed prior organisation, and out of his group of mates, Andy was the main one who sought them out.

Through anonymous sellers in clubs, friends, and more or less anyone he met, Andy explored opportunities for linking into ready sources. It was in this constant quest for seeking out sources that connections were made with certain people which in turn facilitated expansions in his selling. This was the case with meeting Joe. Gaining access to Joe gave Andy contact to a full-time dealer whom he could phone up at any time to place an order. This meant he could act as a reliable go-between seller to his friends and make money doing so. Andy's dedicated commitment to securing drug supplies can be viewed alongside his employment status. For the most part this was low-paid, menial work, and for which he found little energy. During the time I socialised with Andy, he worked as a car valet, as a warehouse storeman, and as a van driver. He didn't make much money from being a go-between, but it was a useful financial addition, and anyway he enjoyed the busy activity and socialising that surrounded it.

There was a further shift upwards in Andy's selling a few years after he linked in with Joe. This was when he began selling out at Venus Group parties. For some time Andy continued to operate cautiously making just small amounts of money, and passing on bigger deals for others to take care of. At a certain point his financial situation was getting worse rather than better, and Andy moved to selling out in more public spaces. These were mainly Venus Group parties, where he knew the security and a fair amount of the crowd too, but this was a riskier style of position to take. This coincided with the point when Rex was presenting opportunities to some of the young men in Robin's extended group to make a bit of money selling and he extended the offer to Andy. In the same way Andy's earlier increase in selling was assisted by forming a relationship with Joe and the privileged connection to drugs that gave him, this further shift to selling out at dance parties was linked to forming a particular relationship with Rex.

Through his regular socialising at the Pace Bar, at Venus Group parties and among the large social network including Robin and Nathan, Andy had become friendly with Rex. Rex bought ecstasy tablets in bulk amounts and knowing Andy, he was prepared to front him an amount on the sale or return facility. The sale or return facility made it possible for people to engage in a higher level of selling than they were otherwise able to. This was because an outlay of cash didn't have to be made. Rex fronted Andy the tablets at £7 per tablet and Andy could sell them at £10, thereby making a profit of £3 per tablet. He didn't sell many; maybe eight to ten at a party but it was all money, and money was what Andy needed.

Convenience purchasing and subsidising recreational drug use

A slightly different way people scaled-up in terms of their drugs purchasing and selling patterns was where they made occasional bulk purchases of 100 ecstasy tablets, or an ounce, or two of cocaine simply because of the convenience aspect. This cut down on the search time for drugs and the multiple exchange arrangements usually required.

Tony was someone who made bulk purchases of cocaine, usually at Christmas. This coincided with when he was realistically able to use drugs. Tony held down a serious job in a merchant bank and because of heavy work commitments, for most of the year was forced into a modest style of drug use. Tony had landed on his feet with his job in the city. He had high ambitions. Banking was going to make him money. He wasn't going to sacrifice it by overdoing the clubbing and cocaine like he had when he was a student. But, every now and then he let his hair down in terms of going out, and the typical time for this was the Christmas and New Year period. This was always a period of high socialising in the clubbing calendar and for Tony it was an extended break from his work commitments. Throughout the rest of the year, his drugs purchasing involved small quantities of cannabis and the occasional gram of cocaine, but in preparation for the festive season he purchased cocaine in bulk amounts.

Tony was loosely linked to Andy's friendship group. This was through Andy's good friend Max. Max had studied with Tony at university. Andy moved on from his friendship group when he moved up to London in 1994, but sometimes he still went clubbing with them and loyal friendships were maintained. Max put Tony in touch with Andy in relation to a New Years Eve club night Tony was organising, and for any advice Andy could give him. It was through this connection that I also came to know Tony. He was white, aged 23 and originally from Essex.

The Christmas holiday period was always one that required pre-planning in regard to drug purchases. A drugs dealer's availability was variable over this time. Tony was well aware of the hassle with seeking out drug supplies once the holidays were underway. For this reason, he was purchasing in advance. Because of his enforced restraint for most of the year, he was avoiding disappointment in not being able to get what he wanted, and he wanted cocaine. Tony's 1995 Christmas holiday purchase was two-ounces (56 grams) of it. He paid £2,500.

This large purchase was mainly motivated by convenience, but it was also in preparation for the club night. On top of that, it would cut the cost of his use. Tony earned a good income, but his cocaine bill for the holiday period would be high if he paid the full retail price for it. At this time, depending on how well you knew your dealer, it was generally between £45 and £60 a gram. Tony remarked: 'I'm buying a bulk lot in from Steve in Porttown. It's coming in at about £45 a gram'.

Tony made his money back to cover the £2,500 by selling it to friends prior to the party at £50 a gram, and in £20 wraps at the party.

The bulk purchase had meant he'd avoided hunting around for cocaine over the holiday period, and he'd been able to use a generous amount of it at no cost, as well as treat his friends. Generosity like this awarded him a high level of popularity and respect, which was all welcome before he returned to his early mornings, suits and financial City life.

Ray was another person whose drug purchasing patterns were scaled-up for reasons of convenience, and also for cutting the cost of his ecstasy use. His ecstasy bill wasn't that expensive, but with going out each weekend and paying the full retail amount for ecstasy tablets, costs soon mounted up. Ray's venture into bulk purchasing came about in a sort of accidental way. He stumbled across an opportunity in a nightclub and on making the calculations in terms of savings, and an assessment of the risks, he decided the opportunity was worth taking up.

Ray wasn't linked to any of the friendship groups I socialised among. He was someone I'd previously worked with, and one night in the later months of 1994 when I was out at Club London with Colin and Andy, we bumped into Ray. Like many others he'd been drawn into the London club scene and was having a great time in it. He'd met a young girlfriend and with her, was going out clubbing most weekends. I went on to see Ray intermittently over the course of my fieldwork. He remained keenly involved in the club scene and talked at great length about it.

Ray had come to the rave club scene at an older age, and by and large had come to it on his own. He was aged 30 when he first started going clubbing. Many people found themselves still involved in their 30s, but it wasn't common to become a full initiate at this later age. Due to the limited peer association he had in connection to clubbing and drug taking, he was forced to rely on people he met in clubs for his supplies. On coming across a chance opportunity one night in a club to buy a bulk amount of 130 tablets, Ray decided to go for it. Ray met a dealer at one of the club nights he was attending. As well as selling single pill amounts in the way of the club dealer, he was surreptitiously looking for big deal customers should the right person come along. Some people were prepared to take the friendly vibe that existed between rave club participants at face value and entered into drug exchanges with people they barely knew but who seemed as if they could be trusted. This was the case with Ray in this instance. With the increasing regularity with which he was going out clubbing there was a growing weariness for hunting out supplies in clubs each week. Moreover, the purchase was going to give him with a cheaper rate ecstasy tablet.

At this point the standard retail price for ecstasy tablets was £15 a tablet. In purchasing 130, Ray would pay £8 a tablet. The purchase amounted to an outlay of £1,040. Ray had a good job and had the money. Ray's heightened purchasing and selling activity was convenience driven with a cost cutting benefit attached. He didn't see himself as drugs dealing. He believed unless you were making a profit out of the sales it didn't constitute dealing. He says: 'when you begin to rely on the profits from the sales, that's when it becomes a very different thing'.

The people I have referred to here were not entrenched in social network styles of clubbing in the same way as the majority of people I write about and their scaled-up styles of purchasing were reacting to their less convenient position within the rave drugs market.

Funding habitual drug use

People scaled-up their drugs involvement and were making bulk purchases for convenience, and to cover the cost of recreational and weekend drug use, yet some were expanding their activities to cover the cost of what for some had become habitual patterns of use. Colin was one of these. Colin was someone whose cocaine use, for a while, spiralled out of control and his changing patterns of purchasing were connected to covering the cost of his heavy and dependent use.

Colin had originally purchased ecstasy tablets in single pill amounts or in amounts of around ten at a time, if he happened to come across someone who had extras to sell. But, a few years after I met him in 1993, Colin was buying cocaine each week, and in half-ounce quantities (fourteen grams), plus he'd begun selling it to cover the cost of the large amount he was now using. Earlier, I described Colin's fairly quick progression into a much heavier style of drug use.

Buying cocaine in bulk meant Colin could use it at a cheaper rate, but the difference for Colin was it had become a necessity. He was using a gram and more a day, and even more on the weekends, and with these amounts he could no longer cover the cost out of his legitimate wages. Even though he was paid well and was getting cocaine at a cheaper rate than the usual £60 a gram, his voracious cocaine use was proving costly. The nightclub Colin worked in has been mentioned as a club where the management was closely tied in with drug sales on the premises. It was while working there that Colin's penchant for cocaine escalated and the necessary links for accessing it in bulk amounts were made. He says: 'The bouncers sell me the drugs they confiscate off people for cheap', and Colin made friends with the club's resident 'coke dealer', who also sold it to him at a discount.

Colin could usually purchase cocaine at around £45 a gram, but buying it in bulk meant he could bring the price down even further. When he purchased half-ounce amounts, he got it as cheaply as

£25 a gram. His plan with these bulk purchases was to sell half of it in gram amounts at the usual retail price of £60. This way, the other half (seven grams) was for him, and at no cost. The intention was well considered and with restraint it would have worked, but for Colin's temptation simply got in the way. From their study of cocaine users, Waldorf *et al.* (1991) observed the occupational hazard of dealers using too much of their own supply and referred to it as a 'recipe for commercial and personal disaster' (1991: 101), and this certainly applied to Colin.

Naive recruitment

There was evidence that some people's drift into a higher level of selling could be connected to being taken advantage of by others who were involved in the drugs trade. While all of the people I observed who were selling drugs were doing so through their own choice and decision-making, there was evidence that some were being drawn in, and exploited through other dealers' endeavours to boost their own profits.

The notion of the deliberate recruiting of naive others into drug selling was demonstrated through Rex who saw the financial vulnerability of a few young males in Robin's friendship group. He saw this as an ultimate opportunity to offer them a job selling ecstasy alongside him. Ned was one, who took on Rex's sale or return offers.

Out of choice Andy did too, but it was at this time that Rex also presented Andy with the offer of a nightclub connection where Rex guaranteed he'd 'sell a lot of pills'. Andy relayed the conversation:

> Rex phoned me at home offering a regular slot in a club on a Friday night where he said I'd easily shift 200 pills. The idea was, I'd either pay in advance for the pills and keep the profit, or else he'll supply the pills and I'll pay at the end of the night.

Andy had been around long enough to be fully aware of the high level of risk this carried and remarked 'there's no way I'm doing that'.

In the same way as people like Andy networked in with useful contacts to negotiate access to drug supplies from which he could in turn profit, dealers like Rex networked and nurtured links with useful, but sometime naive people, like Ned, to assist in getting rid of bulk quantities. The networked reality and the functional relationships of the rave club drugs market worked in both directions.

Another example of the way people were recruiting others into higher levels of selling was evident in the situation Robin experienced when she was being coaxed into buying the 1,000 ecstasy pill purchase from the chap she was trying to buy 50 from. The offer was being promoted based on the low price of the tablets per unit if she would buy a larger amount. This was something Robin wasn't the slightest bit tempted to do. Yet it was offers like these that saw some people weighing up the odds between risk and profit and which some were encouraged to take up. Not Robin, as she explains below:

So you didn't go through with it?

No, I had made up my mind once I got out of the car, I started thinking about it the day after, I don't know who this guy is, he is a lot older than me so he is probably doing it [dealing] quite seriously and also a friend of a friend came back and told me that he'd heard I'd been dealing with some big boys. So if people are hearing that who I don't know very well, that is really not good. That is enough to freak anyone out.

One other way it could be interpreted that Robin was being naively recruited was in the way she was asked to sell at dance parties by the organisers. Effectively this was being asked to take on a more formal selling role with higher stakes at play. This meant taking a larger quantity of drugs along to a dance party and identifying herself more obviously as a seller at them. While these requests made Robin feel important and popular, and the status she derived from the role was enjoyed, in some ways the requests could be interpreted as her being taken advantage of. If everything went to plan, she benefited financially, but it was a highly risky role to take on, and not many people in my study had the courage to do it.

This advantage taking was most evident when she was asked by Andy and Joe to sell at one of their club nights. As an incentive the ecstasy tablets were offered to her at the cheap rate of £5 per tablet. Five pounds was cheaper than she'd ever been able to buy from Joe before, and it seemed the only reason for the reduction was to tempt her into taking on the role of seller at their club night. Through the busy networking that was going on among these connected friendship groups, at a certain point Robin had been able to link into Joe's supplies. The decision to take on the risk of selling at these guys' party was hers, but cut rate deals like this and the previous one described, was one way people were unconsciously being drawn into higher levels of selling. This further emphasises the functionalism and exploitation that underpinned some friend cum dealer relationships. While there was a large degree of camaraderie within the rave club culture, drug relationships were also functionalist in nature. The harsh reality of business, profit and convenience were clear for all to see.

Drug selling as a money-making enterprise

An unconscious drift-like process was how most of the drug selling scaled-up among the people I knew. Though, some people made a conscious decision to take it on in a more organised, business-like way.

Even though Joe didn't turn out to be a sharp drugs entrepreneur, there was a definite point when he scaled-up to a more committed and organised form of selling. Joe was selling a variety of drugs at a steady rate, which was carried out alongside his studies, but he decided to withdraw from university for a year period to take it on in a more focused, profit-yielding way. He was already making money, but by devoting more time to it, he could make a lot more. On weighing up the odds, Joe pulled out of university, and overnight shifted from being a student who sold drugs, to being a full-time drug seller.

It needs to be added that Joe's withdrawal from university was also connected to the difficulty he was encountering in managing his studies alongside his free-party lifestyle. Dropping out was also a strategic decision to avoid study failure.

Ben's actions were similar to Joe's where a major life change was made to incorporate his drugs dealing. Ben was introduced earlier. He was not attached to any of the social networks I socialised within. He was someone I met through my employment in the early stages of my research career in 1993. Ben was selling cannabis, ecstasy and LSD to his friends on a regular basis. At a particular point he decided to give up his full-time job as a health worker to run his selling in a more business-like way. Ben was fed up in his job and considered by applying more time and attention to his selling, he could easily match the money he earned through his paid employment. He had straightforward access to drugs through his brother who was himself a dealer. His brother operated higher up the drug selling hierarchy. Ben referred to his brother as 'a middleman who sold to the dealers in clubs'. He was happy to assist Ben in upping his level of operation. He sold to Ben at £5 a tablet, and in Ben selling them on at £10, he was making a considerable amount of money. So, through his brother from one day to the next, Ben's status changed from selling drugs among friends, and friends of friends, to where he was out and about tapping-up customers wherever he met them. Ben socialised out in the gay club scene. This was a highly lucrative scene to be in. The gay club scene was that of cavalier drug use and large numbers of ecstasy tablets were consumed over whole weekends of clubbing.

Ironically eight months after his full-time dealing career began, Ben was caught in possession of 70 ecstasy tablets and three and a half ounces of cannabis and was charged with 'possession with intent to supply'. The case went to the Crown Court and even though Ben was found not guilty, he was informed by his solicitor that he'd narrowly escaped a prison sentence. Unlike Joe's relatively long selling career, Ben's turned out to be a short-lived one.

Looking after friends' drug selling businesses

Another feature that can be pointed to as an example of conscious scaled-up drugs activities, was the way people stepped in to take over friends' selling businesses either temporarily, or on a more permanent basis. Decisions to take this on were entered into for the enhanced financial gain. It could also be said though that these shifts occurred as a drift-like process in line with being entrenched within a drugs culture.

Jackson was someone who every now and then expanded his selling by stepping in to look after Joe's business when Joe was away on holiday. He'd learned the techniques of Joe's selling through his friendship with him. Businesses that were handed over to be taken care of were those with an established clientele, or a core customer base. The reason for handing them over was to keep business ticking over. Closing off a customer's drug supply, albeit temporarily, ran the risk of losing trade. If a customer located a new buying facility in the dealers' absence, then critical business could be lost. Core customer bases were highly valued and dealers put energy into retaining them. The large free-party group were Joe's key customers, but he had around ten regulars who made 50 and 100 pill purchases. These were crucial to his business. Taking care of Joe's business took Jackson to a higher level of selling. This increased the person activity surrounding him, and the quantity of drugs he had in his hands was a much larger amount than he usually allowed. The quick injection of cash was a big help though, and Jackson enjoyed the limelight that was turned on him through taking on the role. It was certainly a change from his usual high-pressure medical training and exams.

At certain times then, Jackson's selling shifted to the point where for brief periods he could be defined as working as a full-time dealer.

Obstacles to moving out of drugs dealing

It was evident that entering into drug selling was a relatively straightforward process and scaling-up occurred with ease and sometimes overnight. Moving out of drug-selling lifestyles though was far more complicated. A noticeable observation made among the people I was socialising with, was the difficulty they encountered in their attempts to move away from drug selling. Some were never heard to discuss it as a milestone, and others constantly set targets for when they would give up, stopping for a few months before returning to it again.

Mick was one person who was finding his involvement in drugs to be a vicious circle and one which was proving difficult to draw away from. Mick used Rex as a model of someone he didn't want to be. He had got to know Rex through the Pace Bar where both of them regularly socialised. Rex was in his early 40s and had been selling ecstasy, speed and cannabis for some years. A result of being entrenched in drug selling for as many years meant he regularly consumed them, looked bad for it, and often spent his time sitting around in bars and pubs whiling away the hours drinking pints and waiting for a chance sale. The sadness of Rex's way of life, as Mick viewed it, in addition to the prospect of a long career as a drugs dealer was something Mick wasn't keen on. Mick was aged 24 when he was making these comments, which effectively gave him plenty of time before he was on the same par as Rex. Regardless, he was certain he didn't want to end up in the same situation: 'I don't want to be doing what Rex is doing in 10 years time'.

Over the space of two years Mick tried various strategies to reduce his level of dealing. On one occasion in 1998 when he'd just returned from a lengthy holiday abroad and was feeling like he'd had a new lease of life, he said: 'I'm giving it up. I might have to stick with it for a while until I get something else sorted out, but I'm stopping. I've had enough'. Mick's situation typified the difficulties encountered with ceasing drug selling, especially for those who had taken it on, on a more full-time basis. Even though Mick was employed in a café, thereby having an income, small as it was, selling drugs had been a main source of earnings for him for the past six years. It was money which he'd come to rely on. He was well aware of the difficulties confronting him in attempting to replace his selling with legitimate employment. It was his view that 'there's no decent jobs for intelligent young men without degrees', and for this reason he saw himself as being 'in a trap'. His drug sales provided him with a minimum income of £150 a week, plus a personal supply of cocaine and other drugs he could generously share among his friends, and it was a lifestyle to which he had become accustomed. At the point I finished my fieldwork in 1998, and eighteen months after Mick was expressing his interest in withdrawing from the selling lifestyle, he was still involved.

Similar difficulties were experienced by Joe in his pulling out of his dealing lifestyle. Joe returned to complete his university studies in 1995 after his year out, and during his year back studying he was making real efforts to pull back from dealing. It was more difficult than he had assumed, both because of the number of people who relied on him for their supplies, and because of the soft character he was. Andy was picking up on Joe's wishes to pull out, but at the same time the difficulties in doing so. Andy continued to get his small amounts of cannabis, speed and ecstasy pills from Joe. After one of their exchanges, Andy relayed the tactics Joe was using in his withdrawal:

He's been running his business down since Christmas. He didn't want to meet me at his house last night. He wanted to meet in a pub. He used to have a lot of people going through his flat but that's all stopped now. He's telling people this is his last nine bar (nine ounce block) and he won't have anything available after that.

Andy did, though, explain Joe's ambivalence about pulling out altogether. This was spoken about in business terms with the added comment, why would you close down a successful business?

> Basically it's a business that he's built up over time and he doesn't really want to lose it. He's built up these networks around the country. He basically knows what drugs are being taken in places like Sealsford because he supplies someone in that area, and that person supplies in the area. What usually happens is you pass it on to someone else and they look after it for you. You don't just run it down completely, like you don't close a business unless it's not making money. Last time he did this he handed it on to Jackson.

Joe did return to full-time dealing on completing his studies in 1996, but he also held on to longer-term career plans. He chipped away at these and in 1998 he was awarded a place on a professional media training course. That was found to be the right time to really shed customers and move on to something different.

Continued demand from friends

Robin was also finding the drug-selling cycle difficult to break away from. She had enjoyed the centre-stage role her drug selling provided, yet the cumulative negative health, financial, and legal risks were motivating her to give it up. Plus the encounter she'd had with the higher-level dealer was the nail in the coffin. Though, as she points out in the following comment, because of the continued demand from friends, and the money, it wasn't that straightforward:

> You say one more, but it is just so easy to do, like I won't do anything and I will go for a few weeks and then another party will come up and people will say 'oh can you maybe get any pills' or whatever and because they can't get off anyone else and not good stuff as well. And there is no point me doing five and then by the time someone wants five I have got another person wanting five, so it is quite difficult to break out of because you have the opportunity to make money.

Careless accounting

In discussing the difficulties with stopping selling, Robin referred to the free-form style of accounting she had got into. She was paying an amount out for a supply but she wasn't holding back the money collected from the sales to replenish what had initially been paid out. She was making money through her selling, but she was failing to balance her books at the end of the week's selling. This would then lead to another purchase being made with the intention of paying back the amount that time around, though the same bad habit remained:

> I keep saying to myself after every time I pick up 50 pills, alright I am not doing it again, I am not doing it again because of the risks involved but the way I never actually replace the money, I have just constantly got money coming in, I mean I wouldn't have a clue how much I make and whatever I do grab, I usually go and spend straight out.

Drugs arrests

For a few unlucky others, decisions to cease selling were in some respects made for them. This was on being caught in possession of one, or other of the drugs rave clubbers were taking, but it was apparent that even being caught didn't entirely deter. This was evident with Ian as already written about. The sheer volume of people participating in the London rave club scene and the number of venues across London where drug use and drug selling was occurring meant the task of the police in disrupting anything but a small part of it was huge. Rave clubbers knew this, and continued their chances even when they had been caught.

Jamie, Ben, and Ian were three people who were arrested during the time I was socialising alongside them for their possession of varying quantities of ecstasy, speed, cocaine, cannabis and cash. Aside from Ian, all of them ceased the drug selling they had been involved in, but they weren't about to stop taking drugs. They merely devised other ways of obtaining them.

The longer a person was involved in dealing the greater the risk of being caught became, or the sense that they might be caught. It was not only they who had to watch their actions but those they dealt with could put them at risk. There was a point in 1996, not long after Joe resumed his selling after finishing university, when his higher-level dealer was busted. This put Joe into a serious state of panic. It coincided with a time when he was attempting to get out of the whole game anyway and was a scenario that drove him that bit nearer to giving up. Jamie relayed the scenario to me after Joe had visited him in his workplace in a state of concern over it. He said:

> Joe visited me at work the other day. He was running scared. His dealer's been busted with £2,000 cash and 70 Es. Joe thinks he's been watched for a while. He [Joe] had all his drugs in his bag; a lot of grass, coke, Es, and speed. He was off to stash it somewhere.

It was two weeks later when I spoke to Joe himself about his dealer being busted:

> I was really paranoid for about a week because I've been buying off him for a while. The police took his mobile and I'm sure my number's in its memory. I've convinced myself now it isn't. He'll definitely do time inside. He was caught with 70 Es and £1,600[1] worth of cash.

Girlfriends as an influence

Being caught was one way people reassessed their involvement in drugs dealing and pulled out. Girlfriends of dealers could sometimes also be influential in a person scaling-down their dealing, or attempting to move away from it. Lizzie relayed how she had had a 'serious chat' with Jackson about his selling. She was getting fed up with coming home and finding his customers in their living room. Jackson was in the last stages of qualifying as a medical doctor and was mainly selling to generate some fast cash. He knew that not far down the line he would command a decent income from his job as a doctor. The money, therefore, was not as big a pull for him as it was for others. Not wanting to jeopardise his relationship further, Jackson agreed to tone his dealing down. Others were wholly reliant on the income from their drug selling, in which case the decision for them to stop selling was a tough one, even if there was a girlfriend threatening the end of the relationship.

There was a point at which Mick was using a new relationship he was in to facilitate his scaling-down. It took a special temperament to withstand a relationship with a dealer and Mick knew this. He began presenting himself with a different identity of being in a committed couple relationship and having dinners out and nights in. This was alongside toning down his image of busy socialising and being ready and available for people wanting to purchase. As it turned out, the relationship didn't last long and very soon his selling lifestyle slipped back to what it had been before getting together with his girlfriend.

Around this time I had the opportunity to ask Mick what type of influence girlfriends could have on a person's dealing decisions. He responded: 'it depended on what came first, the dealing or the girlfriend'. From this he meant if a girlfriend chose to get together with him in his current role as someone who sold drugs, then it would've been their choice and therefore they presumably didn't mind. To him though, if the dealing role was taken on and cultivated within a relationship where it hadn't previously been, then dissatisfaction from the girlfriend could reasonably be expected. Mick spoke from experience. A previous long-term relationship had broken down in part connected to the start of his more committed drugs-dealing career.

It became increasingly clear that a meaningful alternative to drug dealing had to be found in order for the people I had come to know to consciously quit. Preferably, the meaningful alternative would provide the same level of income as had been yielded through their drugs dealing.

Although opportunities to replace the level of income Joe had been earning selling drugs was not going to be provided through the training programme he was accepted onto, the prestige and the future opportunities it would open up, made it beneficial to quit.

Alternative identities

The notion of 'identity reverting' is a useful one to draw upon in understanding the way people could move on from former so-called deviant lifestyles such as drug selling. This was a concept put forward by Biernacki (1986) in his discussion on the process of breaking away from drugs addiction. Biernacki argued it was less problematic for those who had managed to maintain a good relationship with people not involved in the world of addiction. He also discussed breaking away in the context of 'transforming identity', for example from a drug addict to someone else. Here he said people who created new identities for themselves or reverted to an identity they had held before living in the drug addict world were more likely to be successful. This concept can also be linked with Waldorf *et al.*'s (1991) discussion on cocaine sellers exiting the cocaine world. They argued it was easier for the cocaine sellers they studied to exit the cocaine world if they had maintained a stake in what was referred to as a 'conventional identity' (1991: 222) such as through work or family roles.

To an extent, this situation was observed in my fieldwork. Those who had alternative identities could more easily make the move away from an involvement in drug selling. This could be applied to Robin, Jackson and Tony in that the bulk of their time was spent in a conventional identity. For Jackson this was entrenched in a world of medical training and serious responsibility, and for Robin and Tony it was within their employment in the banking sector in the City of London. This could also be applied to Joe. Even though Joe spent the best part of four years operating as a drugs dealer, through succeeding in gaining his university degree and continuing to pursue career opportunities in the legal jobs market, at the point he felt ready, he was able to revert to a more conventional lifestyle. To this end, exiting drug selling careers can in part be linked to socio-economic and social class positioning. It was those from more privileged, middle-class backgrounds such as Jackson, Joe, Colin,[2] and to an extent Robin and Tony who had alternative options they could draw upon. This was unlike Andy and Mick who were more constrained in their alternatives due to their less qualified backgrounds and the lower levels of social capital they held as a result.

Summary

What these examples have illustrated is the ease with which people could scale-up within the drug-selling hierarchy. It was apparent that people's original selling patterns and intentions may have incorporated only selling to friends, but, as more and more people were met who required a supply of drugs and the initial fears of drug selling had been put aside, selling in larger quantities and to unknown others soon became a part of a number of people's selling patterns. Where for many this occurred in an unconscious, drift-type process, others made conscious decisions to increase their involvement in drug selling for purposes of profit-making and income generation.

Entering into drug selling was a relatively straightforward

process, but exiting was a different matter. Some were never heard to discuss it as a target while others revealed a dependence on the income, the continued demand for drugs from friends, and the lack of alternative options, as a hindrance. One factor that did facilitate exiting was being caught in possession of one or other of the dance drugs.

Notes

1 Note the difference in the cash amount relayed by Joe, to that stated by Jamie. This is an example of the way story detail can become twisted from one person to another.
2 Colin went on to invest in vocational training that established him as an audio-visual technician from which he could operate competitively within the legitimate job sector.

Chapter 8

Later lives and conclusions

> . . . heavy recreational users are familiar with the fluid and
> networked nature of the drug market whereby suppliers can
> extend outward from close proximity – from a friend and a
> friend of a friend – to people you sort of know to just faces
> you see regularly in pubs and clubs . . . (South 2004: 535)

This book has been centrally concerned with the way drugs
purchasing and selling was organised within the London rave
club culture in the mid to late 1990s; a period of much drug use
and trading activity. It has focused on the distribution of drugs
as it occurred within public spaces such as nightclubs and dance
parties, and within the private arena, as social network systems of
operation. In this final chapter the stories are drawn to a close by
firstly providing further longitudinal detail on some of the people
my field observations were based upon. Following that, the main
themes framing the study findings are summarised and discussed.
These centre on enterprise and entrepreneurship, friendship and
functionality in the London urban setting, and the fluid self-
identities of late-modern lifestyles.

Some years have now passed since the completion of my research.
Even so, I am able to note the circumstances of a few people beyond
the fieldwork period of observation. This was made possible through
my ongoing presence among some of the friendship networks in
the years that followed my official fieldwork. This approach can be
linked to a point made by Watson (1999) on the way anthropologists
often return to the field to further enlighten their original studies. In

this way, fieldwork is referred to as 'temporal' and 'leaving the field' viewed as a process over time. In the context of my study, it related to the nature of the ethnographic research role I employed. I was connected to the key characters and friendship networks through friendship, and these were not friendships that ceased on the close of my fieldwork. My exit from the rave club culture meant I became detached from these people's everyday social lives, yet I continued to live and socialise in the north London area and on the periphery of some of the social networks described. With that, in an informal way I remained in touch and familiar with some of their later drug using and selling lifestyles.

In the following section I draw on this extended relationship to note what the key characters went on to do beyond my period of study, where that information is known. Some of this was gleaned from accounts passed on by other network members. This assists an understanding of the drug using and selling careers of a sample of primarily young people as they aged through their 20s and into their 30s. Moreover, it is an indication that rave club drug using lifestyles were unfolding into much longer drug use histories. I begin with the six key characters before discussing other people on whom my account is constructed.

Later lives

At the time of writing Colin was aged 41 and continued to live in London. Following his four years of working as a bar manager in the commercial rave nightclub, Colin went on to pursue a professional qualification in audio-visual technology. This established him in a specialised work role from which he has earned a good income. Colin continued to have a keen enthusiasm for the nightclub drugs culture and for most of the years up to the point of writing, has combined daily life with regular drug taking out in London nightclubs. Some years ago, Colin's cocaine use again began to cause problems, leading to the realisation that it needed confronting, and even quitting. This was a testing time as Colin spent long periods abstaining and attending drugs relapse counselling sessions. This was mostly alongside resisting burning temptations to throw caution to the wind, and go out clubbing and take the cocaine and ecstasy he so enjoyed doing.

I kept in contact with Andy for a couple of years after the end of my fieldwork. He kept up his busy rave club socialising and frequent drug taking, DJing in various clubs and bars, and partying out among different clubbing networks. Plus, he was eventually successful at moving into legal employment within the sphere of rave music distribution. Andy remained living in London for a few years, before leaving to live in Australasia. There he was also successful at picking up work in the rave club economy, on a rave music radio station, and DJing in various rave club settings. This is an illustration of the global spread of the rave club culture and its development in other cities and countries across the western world (Silverstone 2003). Some years prior to the point I am writing about here, I came across one of Andy's original friendship group on the streets of north London. He was now aged 31, continued to live in his home area in the suburbs of south London, and said he still enjoyed going out and 'taking the odd cheeky E'. He remained in contact with Andy, albeit on a long-distance basis.

Due to my relatively detached links with Joe's free-party group, I rarely saw Joe on my exit from the London rave scene, although I did hear about him. He took up his professional training, wound his drugs dealing right down, and partied out occasionally. Around four years prior to the point of writing I came across Joe, also on a north London street. He was 31, lived in south London and was in full-time employment. Referring to the period of his free-party socialising and when I occasionally partied out with him, he commented 'a lot has changed since then'. He was in regular contact with Andy and had visited him out in Australasia on a few occasions.

Joe retained contact with some of the free-party group, but most had moved on to live in other parts of England, be parents, to hold down job responsibilities and generally to live quieter lives. Joe had though become closely linked to Rex and Mick. They regularly met up in pub drinking sessions to watch football. The interesting point with this three-way friendship was that it had been purely instigated by Andy during the period of my fieldwork in the late 1990s. As a part of Andy's busy mover way of life he facilitated useful drug links between others and he had helped engineer links between Joe, Rex and Mick. Whether drug selling continued to underpin the friendship seven years after they'd originally met was not something I was able to elicit through my street meeting. However, the way they had initially come from unconnected friendship networks and largely came together for reasons of drugs trading was an illustration of the networked reality of the rave dance drugs market.

A central finding from my study was the social networked reality of drugs distribution within the rave culture as friends put friends in touch with useful drugs contacts and certain relationships were nurtured based on the ease of drugs supply within them. While drug contacts could be fluid, fickle and sometimes functional, they could also become solid and sustained over a number of years.

In line with these socially engineered drug contacts being a feature of the rave drugs market, Rex took over Joe's drug-selling business when Joe pulled out in 1998. Rex simply added Joe's core customers to his already established customer base. On the occasion of running into Joe on the street, he was on his way to meet Rex in a nearby pub and invited me to join. I had also not seen Rex for a number of years. He was aged in his late 40s and was living a relaxed lifestyle in north London. He combined this with spending block periods of time at a fixed holiday location abroad in the sun with his girlfriend. He was no longer involved in dance party drug selling, though I was unable to gauge whether the same could be said in regard to his social network selling.

Robin returned to Australia at the end of 1998 after her two-year stay in London, and on the last occasion I was in contact with her, a year or so after she departed, she was living in Sydney and making in-roads into a career in the film industry. Few of the London-based members of her friendship network, such as Andy and Rex, maintained contact with her on her return to Australia.

Mick continued living in London. Every now and then I ran into him in different pubs that members of the large Pace Bar social network had started to hang out in. He remained closely linked to his core friends and despite his desire to exit the drug-selling lifestyle, a number of years after the close of my study he was still involved.

Tom, in collaboration with his original business partner continued to organise commercial rave dance parties in and around London. In line with the increasing commercialisation and regulation of the leisure and nightclub-based economy (Chatterton and Hollands 2003; Talbot 2004), many of their event activities were being held in more mainstream venues. In their desire for authenticity some dance parties continued to be marketed in a discreet manner with just those in the know gaining access to details. These were posted through email-based mailing lists and in the same way to that described earlier, location details were not revealed until the last hours.

I had knowledge of other key friendship group members which in regard to drugs involvement revealed a pattern of ongoing drug use and long drug-selling careers. For instance, Rick remained living in London and worked full-time as a bartender. He continued to socialise within a drugs party network and regularly consumed different drugs. He and Anna remained good friends and often partied and took drugs together.

Every now and then I knocked into Stan in my local neighbourhood where he also lived. He had initially struggled with his life of alcohol abstinence, mainly as he attempted to manage it alongside his continued role in DJing, drugs trading and clubbing in and around London. It was not easy to separate the two. On the last occasion I came upon him, some years ago, he was out of the drugs party scene altogether, was working in the field of design, and was on the straight and narrow.

A few years after my fieldwork had finished by chance I came across Jackson on a London high street. He had qualified as a medical doctor and was working in a London hospital. He talked about his problematic break-up with Lizzie and how it coincided with him beginning to use heroin. This led to his arrest purchasing heroin in an open, street-drugs market. With his career in jeopardy Jackson agreed to enter a drugs rehabilitation unit. At the point we were speaking, he was 'drug and alcohol free', but spoke of the struggle involved in meeting up with friends socially saying, 'drugs were never far away'.

These examples reflect the ongoing drugs party leisure culture in the London urban setting and the continued and longer-term involvement of this adult group of drug users.

Recreational drug use and 'cultural normalisation'

It was clear from my observations, as well as from the accounts provided above, that for a number of people involvement in the London rave drugs culture was not simply a passing phase, but rather a much longer period of association (Akram and Galt 1999). Drug-using and clubbing lifestyles were spanning multiple years; varying levels of fallout were occurring, and some people were finding it difficult to put a stop to it, especially those with an occupational attachment to the culture, such as drug sellers, DJs and club night organisers.

The drug-using lifestyles of the people I socialised among were being lived out within the drugs cultural normalisation that was occurring in the UK through the 1990s (Measham *et al.* 1994; Parker *et al.* 1995, 1998). This asserted that statistically drug use was not a feature of the majority of people's lives (Pearson 2001), but the general pervasiveness of drugs in society, and their ease of accessibility in a variety of settings, deemed drug use a seemingly unremarkable aspect of life. This drugs cultural normalisation was the context in which the people I came to know used drugs, and they did not consider themselves as occupying 'subcultural' or 'deviant' drugs worlds.

They viewed themselves as recreational drug users whose drug-using lifestyles were managed alongside everyday work, home and family-life responsibilities. Thus, in a similar way to that depicted by South (2004), they could be construed as 'work hard/party hard' lifestyles (2004: 535). Despite it being the majority who could be defined in this way, for some the lines between recreational drug use blurred with more problematic forms of use. Some of the people within the different social networks I hung out in became heavy and persistent ecstasy and cocaine users, typically, but not only, alongside drugs dealing set-ups. These drugs excesses seriously impacted on their health, plus other aspects of their lives were suffering. For instance, financial debt connected to expensive drugs habits, impaired work and study abilities, and some people, as I have shown, ended up with criminal drugs convictions with lasting and damaging effects.

In this way, it is my argument that the depictions of this leisure culture as largely recreational and unproblematic, to some extent overlooked the real-life difficulties and problems people experienced, and continue to face within today's related styles of night-time leisure. Heavy cocaine-using and drinking cultures emerged out of this rave club scene, which continue to flourish in the London urban night-time setting (Ward and Thom 2009). This combined consumption culture is to date under-researched, but it can arguably be connected to reports of the increased numbers seeking treatment in connection to problem cocaine use (The National Treatment Agency for Substance Misuse 2009).

Ecstasy and enterprise

Alongside the large numbers of people who used drugs in connection to their participation in the rave club culture, there was a large number of people who became involved in selling them. In the same way that drug use became normalised, to an extent drug selling did too (South 2004). As the rave club culture diversified and grew, and with the corresponding widespread demand for drugs, male and female clubbers easily drifted into buying and selling ecstasy, cocaine and other drugs, be this on a low level among friends, or on a larger scale, as commercial, money-making enterprises.

Drugs market commentators have noted how the macro-shift in drugs markets, to large-scale, recreational drugs markets, made it easier for people to enter the drugs economy as freelance sellers and as extensions of friendship group selling (Paoli 2002; Gruppo Abele 2003). Yet, it can also be argued that the readiness to become involved in the rave drugs trade was facilitated by the very notion of this as a recreational drugs using scene that did not carry the same stigma as that attached to trading in drugs such as heroin and crack cocaine (Fagan 1995). Heroin and crack cocaine are largely associated with chaotic, marginalised users and this drug user image was absent from rave club styles of drugs use and dealing. The contrary recreational image debatably enabled dealers to cross a line into drugs trading, while at the same time conceiving of themselves with a particular sense of worth derived from their role in the illegal drugs economy, simply 'providing for friends' drug needs'.

It was without doubt that the drugs culture and drug-using lives of the people on whom my study focused were based on leisure pleasure experiences (Hunt and Evans 2008, Hunt *et al.* 2010), but it is important to add, the drug using lifestyles I observed were not solely quick fix hedonism located within 'time out' lives, but incorporated a range of functions such as providing incomes, jobs, status, and a sense of identity derived from being a member of this unique leisure culture. Alongside nights' out in clubs, the people I observed were entrepreneurial economic actors who used their involvement in drug selling as a form of alternate work, and to some extent paralleled the worth elicited through conventional work roles.

Despite the trade in dance drugs being illegal activity, the people written about in this book who were involved in nightclub and social network drug selling have to be viewed as enterprising characters. They were capitalising on the opportunities being presented to make money within this highly buoyant drugs market, and leisure culture more broadly. Large amounts of money could be made, especially in nightclub styles of drugs dealing as illustrated by Ronnie and Vince in Lush, and Pamela and Ian in Club London and at Tylers nights, but also in busy social network operations. The skill and organisation required to run their businesses reflected that of any business manager. This was in the way they meticulously planned and co-ordinated the range of organisational tasks involved in running a successful business – as well as keeping on top of the financial payments and debts, and at the same time avoiding detection.

It was apparent some had fewer options than others when considering choice and involvement in illegal drugs trading. Aside from a few, the drugs dealers in my study were by and large young people; a number of whom lacked formal education and skills that could be applied in legitimate spheres of work. This was made apparent in the comment made by Mick who defended his role in drug selling on the grounds that there were 'no decent jobs for intelligent young men without degrees'. To these young men, and they were mainly young men, taking charge of a busy drug-selling enterprise was a reasonable alternative to their options in the formal economy. It gave structure and purpose to their daily lives, yielded status and popularity and importantly provided an income.

An additional way I view the enterprise and entrepreneurship occurring within rave club culture was the way nights out in clubs and drug taking could not be divorced from the broader base of this leisure economy. This takes me back to the conceptualisation put forward by Smith and Maughan (1998), where they discussed young rave participants as actively involved in the production of the culture and economy of which they were a part. Rave club participants could be defined as leisure culture entrepreneurs. They drew on their knowledge and experience from within the culture to establish the type of leisure venues being demanded from clubbers. Rave clubbers were involved in producing the rave leisure culture, as well as being consumers of it. The scene I describe in the way Tom and his business partner, and Joe and Andy, among a number of others, were actively involved in creating social spaces such as Venus Group parties and setting up the Pace Bar can be viewed as an underground, freelance branch of the rave economy. This contrasted with the commercial rave club leisure organisation (Chatterton and Hollands 2003). Thus, rather than looking at the consumption of a 'night out' or the consumption of drugs within the context of consuming a leisure pleasure experience, it was more appropriate to look at the broader participatory and entrepreneurial roles people occupied within their rave club lifestyles.

The work in these chapters therefore sheds light on a process at work within the rave club culture whereby young people were effectively creating jobs and incomes for themselves. This needs to be recognised regardless of the fact that many of these job-like openings were located within the illegal sphere of the rave economy. As the life of the rave club culture expanded and the economy building up from it thrived, many of the money-making enterprises turned into longer-term employment prospects, such as DJing careers, dance music record promotion, nightclub decoration, and drugs dealing careers. This thereby meant there was a vested interest for young people across the board in keeping the rave club culture and economy alive. Jobs and incomes depended on it. This can in turn explain the elongated periods during which people were engaged in rave club lifestyles. They were not only participating for recreational purposes, but the paid employment they had established for themselves depended on the ongoing support and participation of their friends, and whoever else they could draw in.

Social network drugs markets and friendship

The drug-selling styles in this book have been broadly categorised as selling in the public domain within nightclubs and dance parties, and selling in more private arenas in social network styles of selling. The six key characters I focused on primarily functioned within social network drugs markets, and it was found that this style of operation could accelerate at a rapid rate. This was as friends put friends in touch with people they knew who sold drugs. Friendship and camaraderie are key constructs around which expansions and accelerations in rave club drug selling operations can be discussed. A large degree of camaraderie underpinned the rave club culture. This was connected to the feelings of empathy and elation generated through the pharmacological effects of ecstasy. It was also through the shared sense of togetherness and belonging created among club crowds and membership in the culture as a whole (Malbon 1999). Total strangers who met in clubs regularly became friends overnight.

Though, I have consistently pointed out that the concept of friendship within drugs purchasing and selling arrangements needs to be scrutinised. Social network drug selling was largely presented as selling to friends and trusted contacts, but it was evidenced in my study that people were referred to as friends in the loosest possible sense. The notion of friends was a useful one to employ. It assisted drugs dealers to downplay their activities based on the fact they were 'only selling to friends'. On closer examination, friendship network customers often comprised loosely connected people who sometimes the seller barely knew. In perceiving of customers as friends, drug sellers could neutralise and dilute the illegality of their drugs trading. Plus, notions of friendship worked from the customer's perspective. It enabled them to ask for favours, such as accessing drugs from whoever they met who sold them. Social and friendship networks were based on strong bonds of friendship, but it was also the case that these were fickle and fluid relationships, based on having a good time and importantly, the usefulness of people in relation to accessing drugs like ecstasy and cocaine at cut-rate prices.

In this way, while rave club drug set-ups were supported by a large degree of friendship and camaraderie, they were also sustained by elements of functionalism and instrumental relationship formation. Although these drug connections were rationalised within the context of friendship, it was evident they were also purposeful, commodity relationships that were being used to one's own, primarily fiscal ends. In this way then, the camaraderie and sense of togetherness can be set alongside the more functional, business-like reality of many drug-selling connections within this leisure culture and economy.

It was without doubt the uniqueness of the London urban context and the nature of social relations and dynamics within a city of London's population size, that greatly contributed to the drugs trading I witnessed. This can be linked to early urban sociological writings which discuss the rational and calculated associations that can occur in the context of large city settings (Simmel 1903 [2002]; Spykman 1926; Tönnies 1955). This also links to Ruggiero's work (2000) that notes the co-existence of illegal and legal opportunity in the context of a large metropolitan setting and the ease with which these opportunities can be taken up.

It is my argument that what I observed in the drug-selling set-ups within the rave club culture was assisted by the relative anonymity and transience that underpins life in a city of London's size and nature (Raban 1974; Ruggiero and South 1997; cf. Greater London Alcohol and Drug Alliance 2003, 2007). This was added to by the sprawling and busy bustle that is a feature of the London setting and was evident in the way club nights went on in unlikely spaces behind dark doors down quiet back streets, and drug exchanges were organised to take place in any manner of situations such as among busy train station crowds and around games of pool in local pubs.

Other cities and smaller towns across the UK were home to a burgeoning rave club culture within which drugs were easily accessed both within nightclubs and social network circles, but the scene I describe is unique to the London urban context. The opportunity and invisibility London offers which I argue facilitated drug selling set-ups, is not paralleled to quite the same extent in other parts of the UK.

Rave drugs market organisation

The rave drugs market described in this book can be set alongside other analyses of drugs market organisation. This is the idea of drugs markets as 'open' and 'closed' systems of operation, characteristically associated with ease of accessibility to the individual buyer (Edmunds *et al.* 1996, see also May and Hough 2004). To date, this idea has mainly been applied to street-level heroin and crack cocaine markets. Open drugs markets are obvious, street-level trading scenes that carry few obstacles for those looking to purchase. Closed drugs markets are ones in which access is limited to known and trusted participants.

The organised drug selling set-ups I observed within London nightclubs such as the resident dealer systems, and the freelance style club dealers in Lush and Club London can be viewed in the same way as the open systems defined by Edmunds *et al.* (1996). London rave nightclubs were open drugs markets. It was possible to turn up at any rave nightclub in the capital at the time of my research and be guaranteed access to a supply of ecstasy pills and other dance drugs. Club drug sellers were plentiful and vigorously competed with each other to shift their supplies. Providing you didn't look like an undercover police officer, club attendees were invited to purchase at will, with no barriers in place and no previous introduction to the dealer required. In this way the rave club drugs market can be conceived of in the same way as open street-level drugs markets.

On the face of it, the social network systems of distribution where drug supplies were largely negotiated through known contacts and familiar links, and the friends of friends chain (South 2004) appeared closed systems of operation. This was backed up by dealers explaining their set-ups 'as only selling to friends', although the person selling would invariably gain financially and was often (although not always) expected to within the friendship network (Ward and Pearson 1997). In addition, as I have described, the idea that social network drug selling was a closed system to known contacts was often contradicted in reality. It was apparent that it was in fact a relatively open one. The links between social network dealers and some customers were tenuous and unfamiliar.

Drugs in clubs and security

A theme that connects to the explanation of nightclubs as open marketplaces is the *laissez-faire* regulation of illegal drug activity occurring within the rave leisure economy. Indeed drug selling within nightclub settings was rife, both in an organised way, as well as in an opportunistic fashion. It was evident that nightclub management systems to some extent attempted to observe the law around drug use and supply on their premises. Door security personnel and surveillance systems were employed to monitor, and as far as possible curtail it, yet it was also evident that a blind eye was being turned. The success of a nightclub could be down to whether there was a drug supply on the club premises, and with this some management systems were complicit in the existence of drugs trade and supply on their premises. This was noted by Sanders (2005) from his research carried out as a member of a security team in a London nightclub. As already indicated in an earlier chapter, he commented that the official line that drugs in clubs won't be tolerated, 'was a façade', and only served to suggest to the law enforcement authorities that they were doing all they could to control drug use within the club (2005: 248). Going further, Sanders found the 'bouncers' who were involved in drug selling within the club viewed their 'unofficial nurturing of drug use as good business'. A drug supply kept the customers coming back and contributed to the overall 'longevity of the club' (2005: 248).

This anomaly can be understood within the dynamics of profit accumulation from within the leisure industry and the promotion of transgression and illegal behaviour (Hobbs *et al.* 2000, 2003). Successive efforts were made to contain and regulate the rave drugs culture and economy,[1] but an ambiguity also occurred. The vast generation of revenue within the nightclub leisure industry was bound up with illegal drugs activity. This may not have been in an explicit way, but it was a very real occurrence in that going out clubbing was all about taking ecstasy and other dance drugs, and clubs that were set up to facilitate it were pulling in crowds and were in the money. This was both in the smaller, underground venues, as well as in official mainstream commercial nightclubs.

The idea of ambiguity in the thirst for profit has been put forward by others. Hobbs and colleagues (2000, 2003) developed this in their discussion of the booming 'night-time economy' and the promotion of carnival-like alcohol consumption practices. They were referring to the seductive marketing employed to attract people to alcohol consumption. It can be argued that a similar implicit invitation to excess was being promoted in regard to drug consumption in the London nightclub scene.

This also takes me back to Silverstone's (2003) work in which he drew attention to the relaxed approach to illegal drug activity within the nightclub leisure culture. He theorised that what was occurring in respect to the rave club drugs culture could be connected to past developments and the way over time, previous illegal behaviours had become tolerated and legalised. To Silverstone we had seen 'an expansion in tolerance to acts that occurred in private' (2003: 211). He argued nightclubs were an example of this expansion. Silverstone wrote 'commercial entrepreneurs had created spaces, overlooked by legislators where illegal practices can go on at a profit' in that they were defined as private spaces (2003: 212).

I contend Silverstone's argument to be a plausible one in regard to the rave club leisure culture and economy. The rave club culture became a key feature of contemporary UK youth leisure and was engulfed by a highly profitable industry (Malbon 1999). It overlooked certain aspects of illegal behaviour in the goals of profit accumulation and successful enterprise. It was evident revenue raised within this night-time economy not only benefited the pockets of leisure entrepreneurs, but also official departments such as Local Authorities and Town Halls (Talbot 2004). Therefore we saw the industry being allowed to continue to operate despite the illegality of some of the activity occurring within it.

Late-modern lifestyles and multiple identities

The style of rave club socialising that I observed can also be discussed within ideas of late-modern society. Alongside the changes that have occurred to societal and economic structures, there is the argument that there have been accompanying changes to our sense of self and self-identity (Giddens 1991). The contention is that in late-modern society we are no longer tied to a self-identity linked to our social class backgrounds. Instead, our lives are lived out within a range of lifestyle choices and options. We are conceived of as occupying multiple and shifting identities depending on how we choose to express ourselves (Giddens 1991; Bennett 1999). In this way, it is considered we have the freedom to attach ourselves to different groups and identities depending on the way we want to shape and present ourselves in diverse contexts. This includes shaping an identity within 'subcultural' drugs worlds.

I argue that what I observed in my study in the way people oscillated and moved between their 'conventional' identities and so-called 'deviant' identities supports the idea of lifestyle choice and multiple and shifting identities (Bennett 1999; Muggleton and Weinzierl 2003). I noted earlier that the drugs lifestyles of the people I socialised among were occurring within a period of drugs cultural normalisation, and therefore were barely conceived of as deviant lifestyles. The reality was, these were illegal drug using and drugs dealing existences which did sit outside of the norms of mainstream society.

To this end, it can be argued rave clubber lifestyles and identities were located in 'deviant' drug user worlds. These were run alongside more conventional identities in home, family and work lives. This was particularly pertinent in the way people occupied serious roles in their daily employed lives, and attached themselves to deviant lifestyles in the form of going out clubbing, and selling and taking drugs in their recreational lives. This was evident with people like Jackson, Tony, Robin and other responsibly employed people. Jackson was located within the high status world of the medical sciences. He combined this alongside a committed and active role in drug selling. Similarly, Tony was employed in the financial sector and sometimes ran his work responsibilities alongside selling bulk cocaine purchases, and Robin worked in the City of London – an image she thought assisted her role as a drugs dealer. In this way it can be argued, the people in my study oscillated between an identity in conventional worlds, as well as an identity in subcultural, deviant drugs worlds.

The above argument does, though, introduce a social class dimension. It was evident that the ease of movement between these two worlds was more accessible for those from privileged social class backgrounds, than it was for those from less advantaged backgrounds. The different individuals on whom my research was focused, and among whom drug transactions and exchanges were occurring, were made up of people of varied ages, and different socio-economic and class backgrounds.

I take on the line of argument that self-identities can be 'freely chosen' (Bennett 1999: 607), and multiple and shifting, but I also take on Giddens' point (1991) that social and economic inequalities still pervade in late-modern society. Identity choice is therefore more of a 'freely chosen game' (Bennett 1999: 607) for those in more privileged socio-economic positions, or from advantaged class backgrounds who have a wider choice of options available to them. The oscillation between conventional and deviant worlds and, moreover, quitting drug-using and selling lifestyles was more easily achieved by those who had alternative identities to draw upon. Some were able to exit drug selling lifestyles through the route of reverting to a more 'conventional identity' (Waldorf et al. 1991). They could fall back on their cultural, social and economic capital and education and skills. This was noted with Joe who returned to his student status and achieved eventual success in a professional career, and Jackson who was able to move back and forth between his medical scientist status and that of a drug seller. This compared to those from less advantaged backgrounds such as Ronnie and Vince, and Pamela and Ian who had fewer established skills and options to draw upon. People like them were more tied to illegal spheres of work and a reliance on selling drugs over the longer-term. Andy eventually found a place within the legal sphere of the rave club economy, but his prolonged involvement generating income, small as it was, through drug selling, was connected to his restricted opportunities in the legal economy.

Rave club participants were enterprising and entrepreneurial actors who took advantage of the revenue raising opportunities available both within the legal and illegal sectors of the London rave club economy. They ran successful drug selling businesses and were engaged in creating nightclub spaces in which the scene was being celebrated. In this way, they were involved in the production of the culture and economy of which they were a part. The rave club scene I have portrayed could therefore be viewed as an interactive, cyclical process in which the culture was being reproduced by rave club participants themselves.

Rave club camaraderie and friendship underpinned the expansive nature of drug selling operations, but friendship was a loosely applied concept which functioned to neutralise the reality of people's involvement in drugs dealing. The busy milieu of the London urban setting assisted in the development of rave club nightclubs as open drugs markets and also in social network markets being less closed than they were perceived to be.

It is well known that rave club culture is a fundamentally different design today than it was when my observations were carried out (Anderson 2009; Measham and Moore 2009). Different drugs have arrived on the scene, and quality and price alterations influence drug choice. Yet, a nightclub and dance party scene continues to flourish in London and the buoyant demand for stimulant drugs, especially cocaine, within clubs and social network arrangements remains. Within the straightforward laws of supply and demand, there are drugs dealers who tap into the economic opportunities presented in these settings and position themselves to cater to this demand.

An assessment of the way rave culture looks today in contrast to when my research was carried out cannot do justice to this multi-layered and varied night-time leisure scene. This would be a study in its own right, and others have made this comparison (Anderson 2009). It is, though, possible to provide a brief overview of where London club drugs culture is ten years on from my research and to point to some differences and similarities.

Where are we ten years on?

The rave club culture of the 1990s was the precursor to the hybrid drink and drugs cultures that emerged across cities and towns of the UK where bars and pubs on urban high streets turned into mini nightclubs and pumped out music, emulating 90s rave club culture. Towards the end of my research, and in the years beyond, these two cultures of consumption – alcohol and drugs – merged as one. The two populations were targeted together and the dual needs of the two groups were served in the same bar cum nightclub venues.

On top of this hybrid culture a more differentiated music and club scene remains. The commercial nightclub sector continues to host club nights with reputed techno and dance music DJs which draw committed club drug users, and venues in more hidden away locations are utilised by leisure entrepreneurs serving the preferences of the underground club music scenes.

The current nightclub music drugs culture certainly does not have the same sense of pervasiveness of the ecstasy culture of the 1990s and early millennium, but there continues to be significant numbers of young and older people who consume an array of stimulant and psycho-stimulant drugs as a part of their leisure lives. Other drugs have emerged on the dance floors and among people's drug using repertoires, such as ketamine, MDMA powder, GHB (Measham and Moore 2009) and an array of legal highs, which are used with different levels of enthusiasm among different factions of the London club and party scene.

Since the late 1990s cocaine use both within nightclub settings and more generally has become widespread. The drugs component of the British Crime Survey is often considered to underestimate the proportion of the nation's population who use illicit drugs, but it has recorded year on year increases in cocaine use since the late 1990s (Hoare 2009). Other information sources report this trend. Cocaine use in London is highly prevalent across different ages (Greater London Drug and Alcohol Alliance 2003, 2007; Ward and Thom 2009). A study carried out with 99 London recreational drugs users, many of whom were active in the London nightclub scene, recorded cocaine as the most commonly used substance among the sample – over 60 per cent were current cocaine users, who used on an average of once a week and an average of one gram in a typical cocaine-using session (Moskalewicz *et al.* 2009). Cocaine-using cultures are emerging in discourses of problem drug use (The National Treatment Agency for Substance Misuse 2009), and are behind comments on the need for drug services to review their design to account for this different type of drugs help-seeker.

The drugs market that trades in these different drugs is very much afloat. In much the same way as reported in the previous chapters there are sellers who position themselves as friendship network providers, and those who capitalise on the demand for drugs within leisure and nightclub venues.

The typology of nightclub drug sellers I provided in Chapter 4 is not likely to be replicated today. Surveillance and monitoring systems in commercial nightclubs will be a deterrent to freelance and opportunistic club dealers, although drugs demand is usually responded to by supply mechanisms. Drug markets adapt to the demand for different drugs in different settings. This was apparent at the time of my research when nightclub and dance party drug sellers began to include cocaine among the stocks they had available. It was also evident in the way drugs dealers positioned themselves in diverse locations, such as in bars and pubs where the patrons drinking in those venues may have been potential buyers. Markets spring up and operate where there are customers. It is therefore likely some form of drugs trading set-ups are in place in clubs where the potential profits outweigh the risks of being caught.

Mobile phones have altered drugs trading beyond recognition. At the beginning of my field observations in 1993 virtually nobody had mobile phones. Landline phones were used to order drugs, and planning and organisation in advance was necessary. Today it is the case that virtually everyone has a mobile phone. Dealers can be contacted wherever they are, and meetings and exchanges can be arranged quickly and around the clock. As a consequence, it is more of a mobile drugs market where purchases are set up to take place at anytime and in any place. That is, taking into account the location of any surveillance apparatuses.

It is the case that a London club drugs culture remains, but that there are diverse recreational drug-using and dealing scenes lived out in all manner of leisure venues and which accompany all types of social celebration. This includes going out clubbing and partying, but drugs taking especially cocaine, is happening hand-in-hand with drinking in pubs and bars, watching football matches, having dinner round at friends' houses, among many other situations. This recreational drugs using and trading activity continues to be supported and facilitated by the busy bustle of the large London metropolitan setting.

Note

1 This was firstly by clamping down on outdoor 'rave parties' and shifting events to take place within licensed leisure venues. It was also through various forms of legislation intended to disrupt drug supply lines within leisure venues. Formal attempts were made to bring nightclub drug selling into line, specifically from the position of door security personnel. The introduction of the Private Security Industry Act 2001 placed the regulation of leisure venue door security under its jurisdiction. All those employed as door security personnel, either through 'in house' arrangements or on contract through agencies are required to have undertaken training and hold a certificate. Criminal backgrounds are investigated. Additional legislative activity in respect to drug selling in certain venues has been contained in the Anti-social Behaviour Act (2003). This enables closing down offending venues without delay.

References

Adler, P.A. (1985) *Wheeling and Dealing: An Ethnography of an Upper-Level Drug Dealing and Smuggling Community.* New York: Columbia University Press.

Adler, P.A. (1992) 'The "post" phase of deviant careers: reintegrating drug traffickers', *Deviant Behaviour: An Interdisciplinary Journal,* 13(99): 103–126.

Akram, G. and Galt, M. (1999) 'A profile of harm-reduction practices and co-use of illicit and licit drugs amongst users of dance drugs', *Drugs: Education, Prevention and Policy,* 6(2): 215–225.

Anderson, T. L. (2009) *Rave Culture: The Alteration and Decline of a Philadelphia Music Scene.* Philadelphia, PA: Temple University Press.

Anti-social Behaviour Act (2003) Closure of premises used in connection with the production, supply or use of Class A drugs and associated with the occurrence of the disorder or serious nuisance. Part One, Section 1–11 (www.drugs.gov.uk).

Armstrong, G. (1993) 'Like that Desmond Morris?', in D. Hobbs and T. May (eds) *Interpreting the Field: Accounts of Ethnography.* Oxford: Clarendon Press.

Beck, J. and Rosenbaum, M. (1994) *Pursuit of Ecstasy: The MDMA Experience.* New York: State University of New York Press.

Becker, H.S. (1953) 'Becoming a marijuana user', *American Journal of Sociology,* LIX(3): 235–242.

Bellos, A. (1995) 'Pay and display', *The Guardian,* 24 October, 2–3.

Bellos, A. (1997) 'The Animal Magic trip', *The Guardian,* 1 April, 8.

Benedictus, L. (2005) 'London: the world in one city', *The Guardian*, 21 January, G2, 2–7.

Bennett, A. (1999) 'Subcultures or neo-tribes? Rethinking the relationship between youth, style and musical taste', *Sociology*, 33,(3): 599–617.

Bennett, A. and Kahn-Harris, K. (2004) *After Subculture: Critical Studies in Contemporary Youth Culture*. Basingstoke: Palgrave Macmillan.

Benschop, A., Rabes, M. and Korf, D.J. (2002) *Pill Testing: Ecstasy and Prevention*. University of Amsterdam, Bonger Institute of Criminology.

Biernacki, P. (1986) *Pathways from Heroin Addiction: Recovery Without Treatment*. Philadelphia, PA: Temple University Press.

Bloomfield, R. (1998) '*Beat surrender?*', *Time Out*, 25 November, 12–13.

Bottero, W. (2004) 'Class identities and the identity of class', *Sociology*, 38(5): 985–1003.

Bourdieu, P. (1984) *La Distinction: A Social Critique of the Judgment of Taste*, trans. R. Nice. Boston: Harvard University Press.

Bourgois, P. (1995) *In Search of Respect: Selling Crack in El Barrio*. Cambridge: Cambridge University Press.

Boys, A., Dobson, J., Marsden, J. and Strang, J. (2002) '"Rich man's speed": a qualitative study of young cocaine users', *Drugs: Education, Prevention and Policy*, 9(2): 195–210.

Boys, A., Marsden, J. and Griffiths, P. (1999) 'Reading between the lines: is cocaine becoming the stimulant of choice for urban youth?' *Druglink* , January/February: 20–3.

Branigan, P., Kuper, H. and Wellings, K. (1997) *The Evaluation of the London Dance Safety Campaign*. London: London School of Hygiene and Tropical Medicine.

Bryman, A. (2001) *Social Research Methods*. Oxford: Oxford University Press.

Calafat, A., Fernandez, C., Juan, M., Anttila, A., Bellis, M., Bohrn, K., Fenk, R., Hughes, K., Kerschl, A., Kokkevi, A., Kuussaari, K., Leenders, F., Mendes, F., Siamou, I., van de Wijngaart, G. and Zavatti, P. (2004) *Cultural Mediators in a Hegemonic Nightlife: Opportunities for Drug Prevention*. IREFREA. (www.irefrea.org).

Calafat, A., Stocco, P., Mendes, F., Simon, J., van de Wijngaart, G., Sureda, M., Palmer, A., Maalste, N. and Zavatti, P. (1998) *Characteristics and Social Representation of Ecstasy in Europe*. IREFREA & European Commission.

Carter, H. (2003) 'Tight security and changing fashion squeeze out drugs', *The Guardian*, 5 December.

Chatterton, P. and Hollands, R. (2003) *Urban Nightscapes: Youth Cultures, Pleasure Spaces and Corporate Power*. London: Routledge.

Chivite-Mattthews, N., Richardson, A., O'Shea, J., Becker, J., Owen, N., Roe,

S. and Condon, J. (2005) *Drug Misuse Declared: Findings from the 2003/04 British Crime Survey: England and Wales.* (www.homeoffice.gov.uk).

Collin, M. (1997) *Altered State.* London: Serpents Tail.

Condon, J. and Smith, N. (2003) *Prevalence of Drug Use: Key Findings from the 2002/2003 British Crime Survey,* Home Office Research Findings 229. London: Home Office.

Criminal Records and Security Industry Unit (2005) *Full Regulatory Impact Assessment: Regulations to Implement the Private Security Industry Act in Respect of Door Supervisors and Vehicle Immobiliser.* (http://www.homeoffice. gov.uk/documents/ria-door-supervisors).

Curcione, N. (1997) 'Suburban snowmen: facilitating factors in the careers of middle-class coke dealers', *Deviant Behaviour: An Interdisciplinary Journal,* 18: 233–253.

Davis, W.R., Johnson, B.D., Randolph, D. and Liberty, H.J. (2005) 'Gender differences in the distribution of cocaine and heroin in central Harlem', *Drug and Alcohol Dependence,* 77(2): 115–127.

Deehan, A. and Saville, E. (2003) *Calculating the Risk: Recreational Drug Use Among Clubbers in the South East of England,* Home Office Online Report 43/03 (www.homeoffice.gov.uk).

Denton, B. (2001) *Dealing: Women in the Drug Economy.* Sydney: University of New South Wales Press.

Denton, B. and O'Malley, P. (1999) 'Gender, Trust and Business: Women Drug Dealers in the Illicit Economy', *British Journal of Criminology,* 39(4): 513–530.

Desroches, F. (2005) *The Crime that Pays: Drug Trafficking and Organised Crime in Canada.* Toronto: Canadian Scholars Press, Inc.

Ditton, J. and Hammersley, R. (1996) *A Very Greedy Drug: Cocaine in Context.* London: Harwood Academic.

Dorn, N., Murji, K. and South, N. (1992) *Traffickers: Drug Markets and Law Enforcement.* London: Routledge.

Dunlap, E., Johnson, B. and Manwar, A. (1994) 'A successful female crack dealer: case study of a deviant career', *Deviant Behaviour: An Interdisciplinary Journal,* 15: 1–25.

Edmunds, M., Hough, M. and Urquia, N. (1996) *Tackling Local Drug Markets,* Crime Prevention Initiative Paper No.80. London: Home Office, Police Research Group.

Engels, R.C.M.E. and ter Bogt, T. (2004) 'Outcome expectancies and ecstasy use in visitors of rave parties in the Netherlands', *European Addiction Research,* 10: 156–162.

Fairlie, R.W. (2002) 'Drug dealing and legitimate self-employment', *Journal of Labour Market Economics*, 20(3): 538–567.

Fagan, J. (1994) 'Women and drugs revisited – female participation in the cocaine economy', *Journal of Drug Issues*, 24(1-2): 179–225.

Fagan, J. (1995) 'Women's Careers in Drug Use and Drug Selling', *Current Perspectives on Aging and the Life Cycle*, 4,(2): 155–190.

Forsyth, A. (1996a) 'Places and patterns of drug use in the Scottish dance scene', *Addiction*, 91(4): 511–521.

Forsyth, A. (1996b) 'Are raves drugs supermarkets?' *International Journal of Drug Policy*, 7(2): 105–110.

Gauthier, F. (2004) 'Rapturous ruptures: the "Instituant" religious experience of rave', in G. St John (ed.) *Rave Culture and Religion*. London: Routledge.

Geertz, C. (1973) *The Interpretation of Cultures*. New York: Basic Books.

Gervin, M., Smith, R., Bamford, L. and Keenan, E. (1998) 'Chasing the dragon: experience in Ireland and association with "Ecstasy"', *Addiction*, 93(4): 601–606.

Giddens, A. (1991) *Modernity and Self-Identity: Self and Society in the Late Modern Age*. Cambridge: Polity Press.

Gilman, M. (1991) 'Beyond Opiates and into the 90s', *Druglink*, 6(6): 16–18.

Gilman, M. (1994) 'Football and drugs: two cultures clash', *International Journal of Drug Policy*, 5(1): 40–48.

Greater London Drug and Alcohol Alliance (2003) *London: The Highs and Lows*. London: Greater London Authority.

Greater London Drug and Alcohol Alliance (2007) *London: The Highs and Lows 2*. London: Greater London Authority.

Gruppo Abele (2003) *Synthetic Drugs Trafficking in Three European Cities: Major Trends and the Involvement of Organised Crime. Final Report*. Turin: Gruppo Abele.

Hall, S. and Jefferson, T. (1976) *Resistance Through Rituals: Youth Subcultures in Post-war Britain*. London: Hutchison.

Hammersley, M. and Atkinson, P. (1995) *Ethnography: Principles in Practice*, 2nd edn. London: Routledge.

Hammersley, R., Ditton, J., Smith, I. and Short, E. (1999) 'Patterns of ecstasy use by drug users', *British Journal of Criminology*, 39(4): 625–647.

Hammersley, R., Khan, F. and Ditton, J. (2002) *Ecstasy and the Rise of the Chemical Generation*. London: Routledge.

Hayward, K.J. (2004) *City Limits: Crime, Consumer Culture and the Urban Experience*. London: The Glass House Press.

Hayward, K.J. and Young, J. (2004) 'Cultural criminology: some notes on the script', *Theoretical Criminology*, 8(3): 259–273.

Henderson, S. (1993) 'Fun, fashion and frisson', *International Journal of Drug Policy*, 4(3): 122–129.

Henderson, S. (1999) 'Drugs and culture: the question of gender', in N. South (ed.) *Drugs: Cultures, Controls and Everyday Life*. London: Sage.

Henry, J.A. (1992) 'Ecstasy and the dance of death', *British Medical Journal*, 305 (6844): 5–6.

Hoare, J. (2009) *Drug Misuse Declared: Results from the 2008/09 British Crime Survey*. London: Home Office.

Hobbs, D. (1988) *Doing the Business: Entrepreneurship, the Working Class and Detectives in the East End of London*. Oxford: Clarendon Press.

Hobbs, D. (2001) 'Ethnography and the study of deviance', in P. Atkinson, A. Coffey, S. Delamont, J. Lofland and L. Lofland (eds) *Handbook of Ethnography*. London: Sage.

Hobbs, D. and May, T. (1993) *Interpreting the Field: Accounts of Ethnography*. Oxford: Clarendon Press.

Hobbs, D., Hadfield, P., Lister, S. and Winslow, S. (2002) 'Door lore: the art and economics of intimidation', *British Journal of Criminology*, 42(2): 352–370.

Hobbs, D., Hadfield, P., Lister, S. and Winslow, S. (2003) *Bouncers: Violence and Governance in the Night-time Economy*. Oxford: Oxford University Press.

Hobbs, D., Hadfield, P., Lister, S., Winslow, S. and Hall, S. (2000) 'Receiving shadows: governance and liminality in the night-time economy', *British Journal of Sociology*, 51(4): 701–717.

Hunt, G. and Evans, K. (2008) '"The Great Unmentionable": Exploring the pleasures and benefits of ecstasy from the perspectives of drug users', *Drugs: Education, Prevention and Policy*, 15(4): 329–349.

Hunt, G., Molloney, M. and Evans, K. (2010) *Youth, Drugs and Night-Life*. London: Routledge.

Jacobs, B. (1999) *Dealing Crack: The Social World of Street-Corner Selling*. Boston: Northeastern University Press.

Jauch, M. (1997) Personal communication – representative of the Eight Areas Clubs and Vice Unit, Charing Cross Police Station.

Johnson, B.D., Dunlap, E. and Tourigny, S.C. (2000) 'Crack distribution and abuse in New York', in M. Natarajan and M. Hough (eds) *Illegal Drug Markets: From Research to Prevention Policy*. Monsey, NY: Criminal Justice Press.

Johnson, B.D., Goldstein, P., Preble, E., Schmeidler, J., Lipton, D., Spunt,

B. and Miller, T. (1985) *Taking Care of Business: The Economics of Crime by Heroin Abusers*. Lanham, MD: Lexington Books.

Karp, D.A., Stone, G.P. and Williams, C.Y. (1991) *Being Urban: A Sociology of City Life*, 2nd edn. New York: Praeger Publishers.

Korf, D.J., Nabben, T. and Benschop, A. (2003) *Antenne 2003: Trends in Alcohol, Tabak en Drugs bij Jonge Amsterdammers*. [Antenna 2003: Trends in Alcohol, Tobacco, and Drug Use among Youth in Amsterdam]. Amsterdam: Rozenberg Publishers.

Lehane, M. and Rees, C. (1996) 'When ecstasy means agony', *Nursing Standard*, 5(10).

London Drug Policy Forum (1996) *Dance Till Dawn Safely*. London: London Drug Policy Forum.

Maher, L. (1997) *Sexed Work: Gender, Race and Resistance in a Brooklyn Drug Market*. Oxford: Clarendon Press.

Maher, L. and Daly, K. (1996) 'Women in the street-level drug economy: continuity or change?' *Criminology*, 34(4): 465–491.

Malbon, B. (1998) 'The club: clubbing: consumption, identity and the spatial practices of every-night life', in T. Skelton and G. Valentine (eds) *Cool Places: Geographies of Youth Cultures*. London: Routledge.

Malbon, B. (1999) *Clubbing: Dancing, Ecstasy and Vitality*. London: Routledge.

May, T. and Hough, M. (2004) 'Drug markets and distribution systems', *Addiction Research and Theory*, 12(6): 549–563.

May, T., Duffy, M., Few, B. and Hough, M. (2005) *Understanding Drug Selling in Communities: Insider or Outsider Trading?* York: Joseph Rowntree Foundation (www.jrf.org.uk).

May, T., Harocopos, A., Turnbull, P. J. and Hough, M. (2000) *Serving Up: The Impact of Low-Level Police Enforcement on Drug Markets*. Police Research Series, Paper 133. London: Home Office.

McCance-Katz, E.F., Kosten, T.R. and Jatlow, P. (1998) 'Concurrent use of cocaine and alcohol is more potent and potentially more toxic than use of either alone: a multiple dose study', *Biological Psychiatry–New York*, 44(4): 250–259.

McDermott, P. (1993) 'MDMA use in the north west of England', *International Journal of Drug Policy*, 4(4): 210–22.

McDermott, P., Matthews, A. and Bennett, A. (1992) 'Responding to recreational drug use: why clubgoers need information, not outreach', *Druglink*, January/February:12–13.

McElrath, K. and McEvoy, K. (1999) *Ecstasy Use in Northern Ireland.* Belfast: Queens University.

McElrath, K. and McEvoy, K. (2001) 'Heroin as evil: ecstasy users' perceptions about heroin', *Drugs: Education, Prevention and Policy*, 8(2): 177–189.

McGuire, P.K., Cope, H. and Fahy, T.A. (1994) 'Diversity of psychopathology associated with use of 3, 4 Methylenedioxymethamphetamine ("Ecstasy")', *British Journal of Psychiatry*, 165: 391–395.

McRobbie, A. (1994) 'Shut up and dance: youth culture and changing modes of femininity', in A. McRobbie (ed.) *Postmodernism and Popular Culture.* London: Routledge.

Measham, F. (2005) 'Drug and alcohol research: the case for criminology', in J. Ferrell, K. Hayward, W. Morrison and M. Presdee (eds) *Cultural Criminology Unleashed.* London: The Glass House Press.

Measham, F. and Moore, K. (2006) 'Reluctant reflexivity, implicit insider knowledge and the development of club studies', in B. Sanders (ed.) *Drugs, Clubs and Young People.* Farnham: Ashgate Publishing Ltd.

Measham, F. And Moore, K. (2009) 'Repertoires of distinction: exploring patterns of weekend poly-drug use within leisure scenes across the English night-time economy', *Criminology and Criminal Justice*, 9: 437–464.

Measham, F., Aldridge, J. and Parker, H. (2001) *Dancing on Drugs: Risk, Health and Hedonism in the British Club Scene.* London: Free Association Books.

Measham, F., Newcombe, R. and Parker, H. (1994) 'The normalisation of recreational drug use amongst young people in north west England', *British Journal of Sociology*, 45: 307–332.

Melechi, A. (1993) 'The ecstasy of disappearance', in S. Redhead (ed.) *Rave Off: Politics and Deviance in Contemporary Youth Culture.* Aldershot: Avebury.

Merchant, J. and MacDonald, R. (1994) 'Youth and the rave culture, ecstasy and health', *Youth and Policy*, 45: 16–38.

Moore, K. and Measham, F. (2008) 'It's the most fun you can have for twenty quid: motivations, consequences and meanings of British ketamine use', *Addiction Research and Theory*, 16(3): 231–244.

Morris, S. (1998) *Clubs, Drugs and Doormen*, Crime Detection and Prevention Series Paper 86. Police Research Group.

Moskalewicz, J., Ward, J. and Thom, B. (2009) 'Quantities, quality, costs and sources', in I. Eisenbach-Stangl, J. Moskalewicz, and B. Thom (eds) *Two Worlds of Drug Consumption in Late Modern Societies.* Farnham: Ashgate Publishing Ltd.

Muggleton, D. and Weinzierl, R. (2003) 'What is "post-subcultural studies" anyway?' in D. Muggleton and R. Weinzierl (eds) *The Post Sub-Cultures Reader*. Oxford: Berg.

Murphy, S., Sales, P., Duterte, M. and Jacinto, C. (2005) *A Qualitative Study of Ecstasy Sellers in the San Francisco Bay Area*, Final Report to the National Institute of Justice. Institute for Scientific Analysis, San Francisco.

Murphy, S., Waldorf, D. and Reinarman, C. (1990) 'Drifting into dealing: becoming a cocaine seller', *Qualitative Sociology*, 13(4): 321–343.

The National Treatment Agency for Substance Misuse (2009) *The National Treatment Agency Annual Report 2008–09*. The National Treatment Agency for Substance Misuse: London. (www.nta.nhs.uk/pulications – accessed 8 October 2009).

Newcombe, R. (1991) *Raving and Dance Drugs: House Music Clubs and Parties in North West England*. Liverpool: Rave Research Bureau.

Norrington Davies, T. (2003) 'Hard work, hard drugs', *The Guardian*, 16 July.

O'Hagan, C. (1999) 'British dance culture: sub-genres and associated drug use', unpublished MSc thesis, John Moores University, Liverpool.

O'Hagan, C. (2004) 'Sounds of the London underground: gospel music and baptist worship in the UK garage scene', in G. St John (ed.) *Rave Culture and Religion*. London: Routledge.

Olaveson, T. (2004) '"Connectedness" and the rave experience: rave as a new religious movement', in G. St John (ed.) *Rave Culture and Religion*. London: Routledge.

Paoli, L. (2000) *Pilot Project to Describe and Analyse Local Drug Markets. First Phase Final Report: Illegal Drug Markets in Frankfurt and Milan*. Lisbon: European Monitoring Centre for Drugs and Drug Addiction.

Paoli, L. (2002) 'Flexible hierarchies and dynamic disorder: the drug distribution system in Frankfurt and Milan', *Drugs: Education, Prevention and Policy*, 9(2): 143–151.

Parker, H. (2000) 'How young Briton's obtain their drugs: drug transactions at the point of consumption', in M. Natarajan and M. Hough (eds), *Illegal Drug Markets: From Research to Prevention Policy*. Monsey, NY: Criminal Justice Press.

Parker, H. and Measham, F. (1994) '"Pick n mix": changing patterns of illicit drug use amongst 1990s adolescents', *Drugs, Education, Prevention and Policy*, 1(1): 5–13.

Parker, H., Aldridge, J. and Measham, F. (1998) *Illegal Leisure: The Normalisation of Adolescent Recreational Drug Use*. London: Routledge.

Parker, H., Measham, F. and Aldridge, J. (1995) *Drugs Futures: Changing Patterns of Drug Use Amongst English Youth.* London: Institute for the Study of Drug Dependence.

Parrott, A. (2002) 'Very real, very damaging', *Psychologist*, 15(9): 472–473.

Pearson, G. (1992) 'Varieties of ethnography: limits and possibilities in the field of illegal drug use', in H.F.L Garretsen, L.A.M. van de Goor, C.D. Kaplan, D.J. Korf, I.P Spruit and W.M. de Zwart, (eds) *Illegal Drug Use: Research Methods for Hidden Populations.* Rotterdam: Netherlands Institute on Alcohol and Drugs.

Pearson, G. (1993) 'Forward', in D. Hobbs and T. May (eds) *Interpreting the Field: Accounts of Ethnography.* Oxford: Clarendon Press.

Pearson, G. (2001) 'Normal drug use: ethnographic fieldwork among an adult network of recreational drug users in inner London', *Substance Use and Misuse*, 36(1): 167–200.

Pearson, G. (2007) 'Drug markets and dealing: from street dealer to "Mr. Big"', in M. Simpson, T. Shildrick and R. MacDonald, R. (eds) *Drugs: Supply, Consumption and Control.* London: Palgrave.

Pearson, G. and Hobbs, D. (2001) *Middle Market Drug Distribution.* Home Office Research Study 227. London: Home Office.

Pearson, G. and Hobbs, D. (2003) 'King Pin?: A case study of a middle market drug broker', *The Howard Journal of Criminal Justice*, 42(4): 335–347.

Pearson, G. and Hobbs, D. (2004) 'E is for enterprise: middle level drug markets in ecstasy and stimulants', *Addiction Research and Theory*, 12(6): 565–576.

Pearson, G., Ditton, J., Newcombe, R. and Gilman, M. (1991) 'Everything starts with an E: an introduction to ecstasy use by young people in Britain', *Druglink*, November/December: 10–16.

Pini, M. (1997) 'Women and the early British rave scene', in A. McRobbie (ed.) *Back to Reality: Social Experience and Cultural Studies.* Manchester: Manchester University Press.

Pini, M. (2001) *Club Cultures and Female Subjectivity: The Move from Home to House.* New York: Palgrave.

Police Foundation (2000) *Drugs and the Law: Report of the Independent Inquiry into the Misuse of Drugs Act 1971.* London: Police Foundation.

Polsky, N. (1967[1998]) *Hustlers, Beats and Others.* Hamondsworth: Pelican.

Power, R. (1989) 'Participant observation and its place in the study of illicit drug abuse', *British Journal of Addiction*, 84: 43–52.

Power, R. (2001) 'Reflections on participant observation in drugs research', *Addiction Research and Theory*, 9(4): 325–337.

Power, R., Green, A., Foster, R. and Stimson, G. (1995) 'A qualitative study of the purchasing and distribution patterns of cocaine and crack users in England and Wales', *Addiction Research*, 2(4): 363–379.

Preble, E. and Casey, J. (1969) 'Taking care of business: the heroin user's life on the streets', *International Journal of Addictions*, 4: 1–24.

Raban, J. (1974) *Soft City: What Cities Do to Us, and How they Change the Way we Live, Think and Feel.* London: Hamish Hamilton.

Ramsay, M. and Percy, A. (1996) *Drug Misuse Declared: Results from the 1994 British Crime Survey*, Home Office Research Study 151. London: Home Office.

Ramsay, M. and Partridge, S. (1999) *Drug Misuse Declared in 1998: Results from the British Crime Survey*, Home Office Research Study 197. London: Home Office.

Ramsay, M. and Spiller, J. (1997) *Drug Misuse Declared: Results from the 1996 British Crime Survey*, Home Office Research Study 172. London: Home Office.

Ramsay, M., Baker, P., Goulden, C., Sharp, C. and Sondhi, A. (2001) *Drug Misuse Declared in 2000: Results from the British Crime Survey*, Home Office Research Study 224. London: Home Office.

Redhead, S. (1993) 'The politics of ecstasy', in S. Redhead (ed.) *Rave Off: Politics and Deviance in Contemporary Youth Culture.* Aldershot: Avebury.

Release (1997) *Release Drugs and Dance Survey: An Insight into the Culture.* London: Release.

Reynolds, S. (1997) 'Rave culture: living dream or living death?' in S. Redhead, D. Wynne and J. O'Connor (eds) *The Clubcultures Reader: Readings in Popular Cultural Studies.* Oxford: Blackwell.

Reynolds, S. (1998) *Generation Ecstasy: Into the World of Techno and Rave Culture.* New York: Routledge.

Rietveld, H. (1998a) *This is Our House: House Music, Cultural Spaces and Technologies.* Farnham: Ashgate.

Rietveld, H. (1998b) 'Repetitive beats: free parties and the politics of contemporary DIY dance culture in Britain', in G. McKay (ed.) *DiY Culture: Party and Protest in Nineties Britain.* London: Verso.

Riley, S.C.E. and Hayward, E. (2004) 'Patterns, trends and meanings of drug use by dance drug users in Edinburgh, Scotland', *Drugs: Education, Prevention and Policy*, 11(3): 243–262.

Riley, S.C.E., James, C., Gregory, D., Dingle, H. and Cadger, M. (2001) 'Patterns of recreational drug use at dance events in Edinburgh, Scotland', *Addiction*, 96: 1035–1047.

Rosenbaum, M. (1981) *Women on Heroin.* Brunswick, NJ: Rutgers University Press.

Ruggiero, V. (2000) *Crimes and Markets: Essays in Anti-criminology*. Oxford: Oxford University Press.

Ruggiero, V. and South, N. (1995) *Eurodrugs: Drug Use Markets and Trafficking in Europe*. London: UCL Press.

Ruggiero, V. and South, N. (1997) 'The late-modern city as a bazaar: drug markets, illegal enterprise and the 'barricades', *British Journal of Sociology*, 48(1): 54–70.

Russell, K. (1993) 'Lysergia Suburbia', in S. Redhead (ed.) *Rave Off: Politics and Deviance in Contemporary Youth Culture*. Aldershot: Avebury.

Sanders, B. (2005) 'In the club: ecstasy use and supply', *Sociology*, 39(2): 241–258.

Sanders, B. (2006) 'In the Club Redux: ecstasy use and supply in a London nightclub', in B. Sanders (ed.) *Drugs, Clubs and Young People*. Farnham: Ashgate Publishing Ltd.

Saunders, N. (1993) *E for Ecstasy*. London: Nicholas Saunders.

Saunders, N. (1995) *Ecstasy and the Dance Culture*. London: Nicholas Saunders.

Shaffer, H. and Jones, S. (1989) *Quitting Cocaine: The Struggle Against Impulse*. Lanham, MD: Lexington Books.

Shapiro, H. (1999) 'Cultures: forms and representations – dances with drugs: pop music, drugs and youth culture', in N. South (ed.) *Drugs: Cultures, Controls and Everyday Life*. London: Sage.

Sherlock, K. and Conner, M. (1999) 'Patterns of ecstasy use amongst club-goers on the UK "dance scene"', *International Journal of Drugs Policy*, 10(2): 117–129.

Silverstone, D. (2003) 'The ecstasy of consumption: the drug ecstasy as a mass commodity in a global market', unpublished PhD thesis.

Silverstone, D. (2005) 'Pub space, rave space and urban space: three different night-time economies', in B. Sanders (ed.) *Drugs, Clubs and Young People*. Farnham: Ashgate Publishing Ltd.

Simmel, G. (1903[2002]) 'The metropolis and mental life', in G. Bridge and S. Watson (eds) *The Blackwell City Reader*. Oxford: Blackwell Publishing.

Smith, R. and Maughan, T. (1998) 'Youth culture and the making of the post-fordist economy: dance music in contemporary Britain', *Journal of Youth Studies*, 1(2): 211–228.

South, N. (2004) 'Managing work, hedonism and "the borderline" between the legal and the illegal markets: two case studies of recreational heavy drug users', *Addiction Research and Theory*, 12(6): 525–538.

Spykman, N.J. (1926) 'A social philosophy of the City', in E. Burgess, (ed.) *The Urban Community: Selected Papers from the Proceedings of the American Sociological Society*. Chicago: The University of Chicago Press.

St John, G. (ed.) (2004) *Rave Culture and Religion.* London: Routledge.

Talbot, D. (2004) 'Regulation and racial differentiation in the construction of night-time economies: A London case study', *Urban Studies,* 41(4): 887–901.

Taylor, A. (1993) *Women Drug Users: An Ethnography of a Female Injecting Community.* Oxford: Clarendon Press.

Thompson, T. (1996) 'Dazed and confused', *Time Out Magazine,* 11 December: 12–13.

Thompson, T. and Doward, J. (2003) 'Ecstasy use doubles in five years', *The Observer,* 28 September.

Thornton, S. (1995) *Club Cultures: Music, Media and Subcultural Capital.* Cambridge: Polity Press.

Tönnies, R. (1955) *Community and Association.* London: Routledge and Kegan Paul.

Tunnell, K.D. (1993) 'Inside the drug trade: trafficking from the dealer's perspective', *Qualitative Sociology,* 16(4): 361–381.

Van de Wijngaart, G., Bramm, R., De Bruin, D. and Fris, M. (1999) 'Ecstasy use at large-scale dance events in the Netherlands', *Journal of Drug Issues,* 29(3): 679–701.

Van de Wijngaart, G., Braam, R., De Bruin, D., Fris, M., Maalste, N. and Verbraeck, H. (1998) *Ecstasy and the Dutch Rave Scene: A Socio-Epidemiological Study on the Nature and Extent of, and the Risks Involved in Using Ecstasy and Other Party Drugs at Dance Events.* The Netherlands: Utrecht University Addiction Research Institute.

Vannostrand, L. and Tewksbury, R. (1999) 'The motives and mechanics of operating an illegal drug enterprise', *Deviant Behaviour: An Interdisciplinary Journal,* 20: 57–83.

Waldorf, D. (1993) 'Don't be your own best customer: drug use of San Francisco gang drug sellers', *Crime, Law and Social Change,* 19(1): 1–15.

Waldorf, D., Reinarman, C. and Murphy, S. (1991) *Cocaine Changes: The Experience of Using and Quitting.* Philadelphia, PA: Temple University Press.

Ward, J. and Fitch, C. (1997) 'Dance culture and drug use', in G. Stimson, C. Fitch and A. Judd (eds) *Drug Use in London.* London: Leighton Print.

Ward, J. and Pearson, G. (1997) 'Recreational drug use and dealing in London: an ethnographic study', in D. Korf and H. Riper (eds) *Illicit Drugs in Europe.* Amsterdam: University of Amsterdam.

Ward, J. and Thom, B. (2009) 'Drug consumption in London –a city of diverse and changing scenes', in I. Eisenbach-Stangl, J. Moskalewicz and

B. Thom (eds) *Two Worlds of Drug Consumption in Late Modern Societies*. Farnham: Ashgate Publishing Ltd.

Watson, C.W. (ed.) (1999) *Being There: Fieldwork in Anthropology*. London: Pluto Press.

Webster, R., Goodman, M. and Whalley, G. (2002) *Safer Clubbing: Guidance for Licensing Authorities, Club Managers and Promoters*. Drugs Prevention Advisory Service (www.drugs.gov.uk/publication-search/young-people/safer_clubbing).

Williams, T. (1989) *Cocaine Kids: The Inside Story of a Teenage Drug Ring*. Reading, MA: Addison-Wesley.

Winstock, A.R., Griffiths, P. and Stewart, D. (2001) 'Drugs and the dance music scene: a survey of current drug use patterns among a sample of dance music enthusiasts in the UK', *Drug and Alcohol Dependence*, 64: 9–17.

Wright, M. (1998) 'The Great British ecstasy revolution', in G. McKay (ed.) *DiY Culture: Party and Protest in Nineties Britain*. London: Verso.

Young, J. (1971) *The Drug Takers: The Social Meaning of Drug Use*. London: Paladin.

Index

Added to a page number 't' denotes a table and 'n' denotes notes.

Aaron 65-6
accounting, careless 140
after parties 61, 62, 63
alcohol 38, 51, 61, 157
  see also heavy drinking
ambience, at venues 23, 37t, 39t, 42t,
    44t, 47t, 49t
amphetamines 10, 53n
amyl nitrate 12
Andy 23, 26, 32, 62, 152
  as an opportunistic seller 76, 86-8
  as an organiser of club selling
    89-90
  friendship groups 26, 37, 40, 42-3,
    63-4
  later life 146-7
  lifestyle problems 69-70
  naive recruitment by 133, 134
  shift upwards in selling 59, 128-9
  as a sustained drug user 58-9
Anna 113-15, 149
Anti-Social Behaviour Act (2003) 53n,
    163n
arrests 140-1
assistant roles 107, 113-15
Australasian group see Robin,
    friendship group

base speed 53n, 55-6, 98
Becky 121-2
belonging 19, 20-1, 153
Ben 83-4, 135-6, 140
bouncers see door security staff
British Crime Survey 10, 161
bulk purchasing 97, 103, 127, 129, 130,
    132-3
business culture 17

calendar celebrations 43, 46
"Californian neuroconsciousness
    fraternity" 9
camaraderie 2, 24, 57, 84, 101, 106,
    153
cannabis 12, 98
capitalism 17
careless accounting 140
Carl 119-20, 121
cartoons, dance drugs risks 14
Castlemorton rave 33
celebration 8, 30n, 34
Charlotte
  assistance in social network selling
    117-18
  rejection of partner 122-3
Chicago School 3
"chill-out" sessions 54
"chill-out" spaces 38, 53n
choice
  in drugs trading 152
  of identity 159
clandestine venues 45
clientele, at venues 37t, 38, 39t, 40-1,
    42t, 43, 44t, 46, 47t, 48, 49t
closed drugs markets 4, 5, 155
Club Cultures 21
club dealers 15, 73-4, 78-85, 91
Club London 37-9
  description, capacity and clientele
    38-9
  drug selling and security 39
  study period and main features 37t
  targeted police attention 80
club squad 88, 91n
clubbers see rave club participants
clubbing 1, 6

extended sessions 61-3
increasing cocaine use 63-6
use of term 8
see also rave club participation
Clubbing: Dancing, Ecstasy and Vitality
  20
clubland 31
clubs *see* nightclubs
"co" drug use 12-13
cocaethylene 68
cocaine
  appearance on dance drug stage 10
  consumption 11, 12, 48, 54, 55,
    63-6, 68, 161
  popularity 64
  prices 63
  ritual sharing 61
  under damp conditions 64
Colin 22-3, 25-6, 144n
  drug selling
    assistance from girlfriend 118-19
    scaling up 132-3
    working with resident dealers
      74-5, 76, 77
  heavy cocaine use 64-5, 67
  later life 146
"come down" assistance 12, 61, 67
commercial nightclubs 11, 33-4, 160-1
  see also Club London
communitas 21
community, sense of 20-1
connectedness 21
convenience purchasing 129-32
conventional identity 6, 143, 158, 159
Cool Britannia 10
crack cocaine 12, 13, 66, 151
"crime as work" 5
Criminal Justice and Public Order
  Act (1994) 53n
cultural belonging 19
cultural normalisation 149-50

dance culture 8
dance drugs
  cartoon sequences of risks 14
  plateauing effect in use of 10
  viewed as being without health
    problems 13
  see also individual drugs
dance scene 8
Davie 69-70

dealer identity 73, 105
dealer-customer relationship 73, 95-6,
  99-100
debt 116-17, 150
detection avoidance 45, 50, 77
deviance theory 18
deviant identity 6, 158
disorientation 69
door security staff 15-16, 73, 76, 156,
  162-3n
dress/codes 37t, 39t, 41, 42t, 46, 49t,
  50-1
drinking cultures, heavy 67-9, 150
drug casualties 37, 77
drug dealers 8
  see also dealer identity; dealer-
    customer relationship; drug
    user dealer
drug dealing 1, 29-30n
drug purchasing
  among friends 15
  on behalf of friends 126-9
  convenience 129-32
  group 86-7
  Joe 97, 98
  in nightclubs 5
  panic buying 82
  in pre-club bar 48
  Robin 94, 97, 127
  Venus Group parties 46
drug sellers
  defined 8
  interaction with 73, 95-6, 99-100
  safety issues 73, 74, 98
  see also club dealers; opportunistic
    dealers; resident dealers; social
    network dealers
drug selling 1, 2
  acceleration/scaling up 15, 59
    convenience purchasing 129-32
    drift process 126
    funding habitual drug use 132-3
    looking after friends' businesses
      136-7
    money-making enterprise 135-6
    naive recruitment 133-5
    purchasing on behalf of friends
      126-9
  as alternate work 5
  among rave club participants 15
  at nightclubs 14-15, 73-90, 156-7

by door security staff 15-16
Club London 39
Lush 41
organisers 89-90
Tylers 43-4
competition 79
ease of entry into 65, 72
friendship groups 2, 5, 15, 92-106
market framework 4-5, 14-16
moving out of
  identity transformation 125-6,
    159
  obstacles to 137-43
Pace Bar 48-9
partnership arrangements 73, 84,
  98
rights 75, 79
safety strategies 80, 83, 87-8, 94-5
Thrash parties 51
Venus Group parties 46
women in see women
drug use
  among clubbing populations 6,
    11-14
  control 55, 70
  emergence of rave club culture 1
  functionality 5, 63, 66, 69-70, 84
  funding habitual 132-3
  health problems 67-70
  normalisation 10, 149-50
  rave club music 32
  research see ethnographic research
  see also illegal drug use; poly
      drug use; problem drug
      use; recreational drug use;
      sustained drug use
drug user dealer 66-7
drugs
  availability and acceptability of 19
  health information and education
    13-14
  quality control 77
  see also individual drugs
drugs contacts 106, 148
drugs market 4-5, 14-16, 155-6, 161-2
drugs snobbery 55

e-heads 55
economic actors/agents 5, 17-18, 32
ecstasy
  availability in clubs 5

club selling 86, 90
consumption 1, 10, 11, 12, 54, 55,
  56-8
diffusion in Europe 9, 30n
and enterprise 151-3
mental illness 69
prices 63, 70n, 76, 131
purity tests 57
ecstasy culture 7-8, 17
ecstasy-related death 13
education, about risks 13-14
electronic dance music culture 8
embodied place, rave club experience
  21
enjoyment, diminishing 96
enterprise 5, 81, 151-3
Entertainments (Increased Penalties)
  Act (1990) 53n
entrepreneurship 5, 11, 17-18, 23, 39,
  49, 59-60, 81-2, 89
ethnographic research 3-4
  drug dealing 29-30n
  "leaving the field" 71n, 146
  rave club culture 1-3, 31
    entry into 22-5
    key characters 25-9
    sites and venues 37-52
    terminology 7-8, 30n
    theoretical foci 4-6
euphoria 68
exploitation 84
extended clubbing sessions 61-3

fluid identities 6, 19-20
free drug recipients 119-22
free-market economics 19
free-parties 36
  see also Thrash parties
friends
  businesses, looking after 136-7
  continued demands from 139
  drug purchasing on behalf of 126-9
  use of term 2, 154
friendship, and selling 153-4
friendship groups 24-5
  drug selling 2, 5, 15, 92-106
  drug use styles 55-67
    extended clubbing 61-3
    heavy ecstasy use 56-8
    increasing cocaine use 63-7
    poly drug use 55-6

sustained use 58-9
overlapping 35-6
sites and venues 37-52
see also Andy; Joe; Mick; Rex;
Robin; Tom
frontline role 107, 109-13
functionality 5, 63, 66, 69-70, 84

garage-music scene 13, 21, 53n
"gay" night clubs, drug use 13
gender relations 19
GHB 161
girlfriends, as an influence 141-2
global phenomenon, rave club
culture as 11
globalisation 19
go-between style 126-8
group identity 19
group purchasing 86-7

habitual use, funding 132-3
hard-core music scene 32, 37t, 42t,
44t, 47t, 49t, 51
"harm reduction" philosophy 13
health information 13-14
health problems 67-70, 96, 150
heavy drinking 67-9, 150
Henley Centre for Forecasting 10
heroin 12, 13, 151
hipness 21
hosts, small venue clubs 35, 43
house parties 104-5
housekeeping-type role 116

Ian 78-82, 91, 140, 152
identity
reverting/transformation 125-6,
142-3
shifting/fluidity of 6, 19-20, 158-60
see also dealer identity
illegal drug activity, relaxed attitude
to 16, 156, 157
illegal drug use 10, 18
income generation 17
instrumental free recipients 121-2

Jackson
conventional identity 143, 158
later life 149
looking after Joe's business 136-7
rejection by partner 123-4

scaling down 141
Jamie 100, 118, 140
partner's rejection of 122-3
Joe 27, 152
drug selling
acceleration/scaling up of 135
as an organiser 89-90
difficulties of moving out of
138-9
as social network dealer 96-101
fear of arrest 140-1
friendship group 27, 54-5, 55-6, 147
later life 147
poly drug use 55-6

ketamine 12, 52, 53n, 55, 98

late modern society 6, 18-19, 20,
158-60
Lee 90
leisure entrepreneurship 11, 17, 23,
39, 49
liberal capitalism 17
licensing, DJ bars 36
Lifeline 14
lifestyle choices 6, 19, 20
lifestyle problems 67-70, 150
lifestyles, late modern 158-60
Lisa 118-19
Lizzie 123-4, 141, 149
London
rave club scene
drug selling 72-91
venues and events 33-52
urban setting 2, 6, 25, 91, 150,
154-5
LSD 10, 11, 12, 52, 55, 69, 88, 98
Lush 39-40
description, capacity and clientele
40-1
drug selling and security 41-2, 77
profits 76-7
resident dealers 74-7
study period and main features 39t

magic mushrooms 12, 55
management *see* organisation/
management
Max 77, 117-18, 130
MDMA *see* ecstasy
MDMA powder 161

mental ill-health 69-70
Mick 28, 44, 147
    drug selling
        defence of role 152
        obstacles to moving out of 137-8
        scaling down 141-2
        as a social network dealer 101-6
        as a user dealer 66-7
    friendship group 28-9, 66, 69
    heavy cocaine use 67
    later life 148
mobile phones 162
"modern system of fraternity" 15
money-making 135-6
moving dance parties 35-6
    see also Venus Group parties
multiple identities 6, 19-20, 158-60

naive recruitment 133-5
naivety 84-5
Nathan 70, 89-90, 110
Ned 57, 84-5, 133
Nicky 119-20
night-time economy 157
nightclubs
    commercial 11, 33-4, 160-1
        see also Club London
    drug selling see drug selling
    as a drugs marketplace 4-5, 15
    small venue 34-5
        see also Lush; Tylers
    see also club dealers; clubbers;
        clubbing
Nitta 81
normalisation, drug use 10, 149-50

older group's drug use 59-61
open drugs markets 4, 155
opiates 12
opportunistic dealers 74, 85-8, 91, 161
organisation/management 32
    moving dance parties 35
        Venus Group events 45-6
    of nightclubs 34, 35
        Club London 38-9
        Lush 40-1, 42
        Tylers 43, 44
    rave drugs market 155
    Thrash parties 49, 50
organisers, club selling 89-90

Pace Bar 47-8, 61, 63, 147
    drug selling and security 48-9
    study period and main features 47t
Pamela 78-82, 91, 109-10, 152
panic buying 82
participant observation 1-2, 3
parties see after parties; free-parties;
        house parties; moving dance
        parties; pay parties; squat
        parties
partnership arrangements 73, 84, 98
partying
    defined 8
    see also clubbing
passive selling style 87-8
pay parties 17
Peanut Pete 14
person capacity, of venues 34, 38, 40,
        43, 48
"pick-and-mix" approach, drug use
        13
police
    detection avoidance 45, 50, 77
    undercover officers 78
poly drug use 12-13, 55-6
post-subcultural theorising 19
pre-club DJ bars 36
    see also Pace Bar
pre-ordering 98
private drug activity, tolerance
        towards 16
Private Security Industry Act (2001)
        162n
problem drug use 64-6, 150
professionalism 82
profit(s) 76-7, 80, 86, 88, 90, 100, 102,
        156, 157
protest, rave club participation as 16,
        18, 49-50
psychological well-being 68
Public Entertainments Licences
        (Drug Misuse) Act (1997) 53n
pubs, drug exchanges in 99

quality control 77

"railway arch" venues 43, 77
rave club culture
    current 160-2
    drugs market 14-16
    ethnographic research 1-3, 31

entry into 22-5
key characters 25-9
sites and venues 37-52
terminology 7-8, 30n
theoretical foci 4-6
as a global phenomenon 11
as recreational culture 70
theorisations 16-22
in UK
different forms 9-11
drug taking behaviour 1
media and public criticism 13
origins 9
rave club music 9, 32, 53n
see also garage-music scene; hard-
core music scene; techno-
music scene
rave club participants 31
drug selling among 15
drug use 11-14
as economic agents 17-18, 32
entrepreneurship 5, 17-18, 49, 152
information exchange between 75
lifestyle and health problems 67-9
rave club participation
camaraderie 2, 24, 57, 84, 101, 106
contemporary youth sociality 19-20
likened to religious affiliation 20-1
as protest 16, 18, 49-50
status and subcultural capital 21-2
see also clubbing
rave club scene
as an interactive, cyclical process
159-60
terminology 8
see also London rave club scene
rave culture 7, 8, 9
ravers 31
raves 33
Ravinda 85-6, 116-17
raving 21
Ray 130-1
reckless drug use 56
recreational drug use 12, 58, 70n,
129-32, 149-50
relationships, urban settings 6
religious affiliation, rave club
membership likened to 20-1
resident dealers 73, 74-7, 91
Rex 28, 44, 91, 110, 129, 147
after parties 63

as club dealer 82-3, 84
friendship group 28, 62
later life 148
naive recruitment 133-4
Rick 113-15, 149
risks
education about 14
of selling 112-13
transport of drugs 83-4, 96, 98-9
Robin 27-8, 44, 143
after parties 63
conventional identity 158
drug selling 90
difficulties of moving out of 139,
140
difficulty in separating business
from pleasure 83
frontline role 109, 110-13
naive recruitment 134
as social network dealer 93-6, 97
transportation risks 84
upward shift in 65, 126-8
friendship group 28, 56-8, 62-3,
65, 94
later life 148
Ronnie 74-7, 91, 152

Safer Dancing campaign 14
safety hazardous venues 41-2, 50, 52
safety issues 73, 74, 98
safety strategies 80, 83, 87-8, 94-5
sale or return 115, 129
secrecy, of venues 45
security
Club London 39
Lush 41-2, 76, 77
Pace Bar 48-9
Thrash parties 51
Tylers 43-4
Venus Group parties 46
see also door security staff
self-expression 6, 20
self-identity 18, 19, 20, 158, 159
"semi-open" distribution systems 4
sense of community 20-1
Simon 81, 85-6, 116-17
small venue nightclubs 34-5
see also Lush; Tylers
social change 19
social class 6, 9-10, 18, 19
social network dealers 92-106

Joe 96-101
Mick 101-6
Rex 82
Robin 93-6
social network selling
  female assistance 117-19
  and friendship 153-5
social pluralism 18
socialisation 10, 56, 60, 61, 68
special calendar dates 43, 46
speed 11, 12, 69
spiritual practice, raving as 20-1
squat parties 29, 30n, 50, 51, 56
Stan 68-9, 70, 149
status 21-2
"steerer" role 115
stigma, drug selling 105, 151
structuralist interpretations 16-17
subcultural capital 21-2
subcultural theory 18
Sunday night clubs 43
super clubs 34
surveillance 78, 156, 161, 162
sustained drug use 55, 58-9

techno-music scene 13, 23, 29, 32, 37t, 39t, 42t, 43, 44t, 49t, 51
temazepam 61, 98
terminology 7-8, 30n
Thatcherism 16, 17
Thrash parties 49-50
  description, capacity and clientele 50-1
  drug selling and security 51
  example 51-2
  study period and main features 49t
ticket prices 34-5, 39, 45-6
togetherness 20-1, 153
Tom's group 59-61, 63, 119, 148-9, 152

Tony 129-30, 143, 158
transformational, raving as 21
transporting drugs 83-4, 96, 98-9
trust 74
Tylers 42-3
  description, capacity and clientele 43
  drug selling and security 43-4
  study period and main features 42t

venues and sites 37-52
Venus Group parties 44-5
  description, capacity and clientele 45-6
  drug selling and security 46
  example 46-7
  study period and main features 44t
  see also Tom's group
Vince 74-7, 91, 152

water, charging for 38-9
women
  and drug selling 107-24
    as active agents 108
    assistant role 107, 113-15
    female attributes 108
    as free drug recipients 119-20
    frontline role 107, 109-13
    as instrumental free recipients 121-2
    practicalities and assistance 115-17
    rejection of partners 122-4
    social network selling 117-19
  and drug use 19
"work hard/party hard" 150

youth culture 10, 18, 19
youth sociality 19-20